DISNEYLAND'S HIDDEN MICKEYS

And Hidden Surprises

. . . .

A Field Guide to
**Disneyland®
Resort's**
Best Kept Secrets

. . . .

8th Edition

Steven M. Barrett

SMBBooks, Inc.

T0027218

DISNEYLAND'S HIDDEN MICKEYS
A Field Guide to Disneyland® Resort's Best Kept Secrets
8th edition

by **Steven M. Barrett**

Published by
SMBBooks
7025 CR 46A, Suite 1071
Lake Mary, FL 32746
www.HiddenMickeyGuy.com

Copyright ©2023 by Steven M. Barrett
Eighth Edition
Printed in the U.S.A.
Cover design by Foster & Foster
Interior Design by Starving Artist
Design Studio
Maps designed by Kevin C. Riley - Updated
Library of Congress Control Number:
2023920686
ISBN-13: 978-1-7342652-4-8

Trademarks, Etc. • • • • • • •

This book makes reference to various Disney copyrighted characters, trademarks, marks, and registered marks owned by The Walt Disney Company and Disney Enterprises, Inc.

All references to these properties are made solely for editorial purposes. Neither the author nor the publisher makes any commercial claim to their use, and neither is affiliated with The Walt Disney Company in any way.

Also by Steven M. Barrett

Hidden Mickeys:
A Field Guide to Walt Disney World's
Best Kept Secrets

Hidden Mickeys Go To Sea:
A Field Guide to the Disney Cruise Line's
Best Kept Secrets

Dedication • • • • • • • • • • •

I dedicate this book to my wife Vickie and our son Steven, who support and help me with my Hidden Mickey passion, and to the many wonderful Hidden Mickey fans I've met through my website and in the Disney parks.

About the Author • • • • • •

Author Steven M. Barrett paid his first visit to Disneyland as a child. He has hunted Hidden Mickeys at Disneyland for years and wrote his first *Disneyland's Hidden Mickeys* book in 2007. Because new Hidden Mickeys appear over time and others are lost, he updates the book every few years. In this book, you'll find a Hidden Mickey Scavenger Hunt for each of the theme parks, along with a third hunt that includes Downtown Disney, the three resort hotels, and other areas on Disneyland property. To organize the Scavenger Hunts for efficient touring, Steve consulted various guidebooks and conducted his own research.

True to their name, Hidden Mickeys are elusive. New ones appear from time to time, and some old ones disappear (see page 18). So, if you can't find a Mickey—or if you're looking for just a few more—be sure to check out my website:

www.HiddenMickeyGuy.com

And our social media: "hiddenmickeyguy" on Twitter (X), Instagram, and YouTube - and "Hidden Mickey Guy" on Facebook.

Thank You, My Fellow Hidden Mickey Hunters

Scores of dedicated Mickey sleuths have helped me find the elusive Mouse. Many thanks to each and every one of you. You'll find your names in the *Acknowledgements*, beginning on page 153.

Table of Contents • • • • • •

Maps

Read This First! • • • • • •

My guess is that you've visited Disneyland before, perhaps many times. But if I've guessed wrong, and this is your first visit, then this note is for you.

Searching for Hidden Mickeys is lots of fun. But it's not a substitute for letting the magic of Disney sweep over you as you experience the Disneyland parks for the first time. For one thing, the scavenger hunts I present in this book do not include all the attractions in the Disneyland theme parks. That's because some of them don't have Hidden Mickeys! (Or their Hidden Mickeys are not visible to the general guest). Therefore, the first-time visitor should get ready for fun by also consulting a general Disneyland Resort guidebook for descriptions of Disneyland attractions, shows, dining, and other tourist information.

That doesn't mean you can't search for Hidden Mickeys, too. Just follow the suggestions in Chapter One of this book for *Finding Hidden Mickeys Without Scavenger Hunting*. **Take note: the newest (to the book) Hidden Mickeys are underlined in the book!**

Chapter 1

Hidden Mickey Mania

Have you ever marveled at a "Hidden Mickey"? People in the know often shout with glee when they recognize one. Some folks are so involved with discovering them that Hidden Mickeys can be visualized where none actually exist. These outbreaks of Hidden Mickey mania are confusing to the unenlightened. So, let's all get enlightened!

Here's the definition of an official Hidden Mickey: a partial or complete image of Mickey Mouse that has been hidden by Disney's lmagineers and artists in the designs of Disney attractions, hotels, restaurants, and other areas. These images are designed to blend into their surroundings. Sharp-eyed visitors have the fun of finding them.

The practice probably started as an inside joke among the lmagineers (the designers and builders of Disney attractions). According to Disney guru Jim Hill (JimHillMedia.com), Hidden Mickeys originated in the late 1970s or early 1980s, when Disney was building Epcot and Management wanted to restrict Disney characters like Mickey and Minnie to Walt Disney World's Magic Kingdom. The lmagineers designing Epcot couldn't resist slipping Mickeys into the new park, and thus "Hidden Mickeys" were born. Guests and "Cast Members" (Disney employees) started spotting them and the game took on a life of its own. Today, Hidden Mickeys are anticipated in any new Disney construction anywhere, and Hidden Mickey fans can't wait to find them.

Hidden Mickeys come in all sizes and many forms. The most common is an outline of Mickey's head formed by three intersecting circles, one for Mickey's round head and two for his round ears. Among Hidden Mickey fans, this image is known as the "classic" Hidden Mickey, a term I will adopt in this book. Other Hidden Mickeys include a side or oblique (usually three-quarter) profile of Mickey's face and head, a side profile of his entire body, a full-length silhouette of his body seen from the front, a detailed picture of his face or body, or a three-dimensional Mickey Mouse. Sometimes just his gloves, handprints, shoes, or ears appear. Even his name or initials in unusual places may qualify as a Hidden Mickey.

And it's not just Mickeys that are hidden. The term "Hidden Mickey" also applies to hidden images of other popular characters. There are Hidden Minnies, Hidden Donald Ducks, Hidden Goofys, and other Hidden Characters in the Disney theme parks, and I include them in this book.

The sport of finding Hidden Mickeys is catching on and adds even more interest to an already fun-filled Disneyland vacation. This book is your "field guide" to more than 415 Hidden Mickeys and Hidden Surprises in the Disneyland Resort. To add to the fun, instead of just describing them, I've organized them into three scavenger hunts, one for each of the theme parks and one for all the rest of the Disneyland Resort: Downtown Disney District, the resort hotels, and beyond. The hunts are designed for maximum efficiency so that you can spend your time looking for Mickey rather than cooling your heels in lines. Follow the Clues and you will find the best Hidden Mickeys Disneyland has to offer. If you have trouble spotting a particular Hidden Mickey (some are extraordinarily well-camouflaged!), you can turn to the Hints at the end of each scavenger hunt for a fuller description.

Scavenger Hunting for Hidden Mickeys

To have the most fun and find the most Mickeys, follow these tips:

*
   If you want to spend the extra cash, pay for the current version of *Disney Genie+* and/or *Individual Lightning Lane* (you'll pay a separate cost for each one) to enter your chosen attraction's Lightning Lane and accelerate your hunts in the parks. You can access these extra services on the *Disneyland* app (it's free to download) on your smart phone. On certain attractions, however, Hidden Mickeys can only be seen from the Standby (regular) queue. You'll miss them if you take the Lightning Lane route. Therefore, to speed up your hunts even more (if you choose to spend the money), I recommend reserving Lightning Lane (by purchasing the current version of *Disney Genie+*) for one or more of the following:
- At Disneyland: *Matterhorn Bobsleds, Space Mountain, Haunted Mansion, Indiana Jones Adventure, Big Thunder Mountain Railroad*, and *"it's a small world"*.

- At Disney California Adventure: *Soarin'* and *Incredicoaster*.

If you don't opt for the Lightning Lane options, just follow my Scavenger Hunt plan for efficient touring.

* **Arrive early** for the theme park hunts—45 minutes ahead of your entry time. If you're eligible for early entry (because you're holding a special ticket that allows early entry or you are staying in one of the three Disney Hotels and have a valid park admission and a park reservation), arrive at the early-entry park for that day 45 minutes or so before the early entry opening time. If you're not eligible for early entry, go to the non-early entry park for that day and arrive 45 minutes before the official opening time.

Pick up a Park Guidemap and plot your course. Find times for shows, parades, fireworks, etc. on your Disneyland app. Then look for Hidden Mickeys in the waiting area while you wait for the rope to drop. You'll find the Clues for those areas by checking the Index to Mickey's Hiding Places in the back of this book. Look under "Entrance areas." You'll notice that headliner attractions are the first stops in the scavenger hunts. If you arrive later in the day, you may want to use Genie+ to book your first major attraction and then skip down a few Clues to stay ahead of the crowd.

* **"Clues" and "Hints"**
Clues under each attraction will guide you to the Hidden Mickey(s). If you have trouble spotting them, you can turn to the Hints at the end of the hunt for a fuller description. The Clues and

Hints are numbered consecutively, that is, Hint 1 goes with Clue 1, so it's easy to find the right Hint if you need it. In some cases, you may have to ride the attraction more than once to find all the Hidden Mickeys.

* Scoring

All Hidden Mickeys are fun to find, but all Hidden Mickeys aren't the same. Some are easier to find than others. I assign point values to Hidden Mickeys, identifying them as easy to spot (a value of 1 point) to difficult to find the first time (5 points). I also consider the complexity and uniqueness of the image: the more complex or unique the Hidden Mickey, the higher the point value. For example, some of the easy-to-spot Hidden Mickeys in Mickey's Toontown in Disneyland are one- or two-point Mickeys. The brilliantly camouflaged Mickey hiding in the tree on one of the ceramic panels decorating a column outside Disney's Grand Californian Hotel & Spa is a five-pointer (Clue 10 in the Downtown Disney and Hotel Scavenger Hunt).

* Playing the game

You can hunt solo or with others, just for fun or competitively. There's room to tally your score in the guide. Families with young children may want to focus on one- and two-point Mickeys that the little ones will have no trouble spotting. (Of course, little ones tend to be sharp-eyed, so they may spot familiar shapes before you do in some of the more complex patterns.) Or you may want to split your party into teams and see who can rack up the most points (in which case, you'll probably want to have a copy of this guide for each team).

Of course, you don't have to play the game at all. You can simply look for Hidden Mickeys in attractions as you come to them. (See *Finding Hidden Mickeys Without Scavenger Hunting* below.)

* Following the Clues

The hunts often call for crisscrossing the parks. This may seem illogical at first, but trust me, it will keep you ahead of the crowd. Besides, it adds to the fun of the hunt and, if you're playing competitively, keeps everyone on their toes. Warning: Many Hidden Mickeys are waiting to be found in the Disney Parks. Depending on the crowds and the park hours when you visit, you may not be able to complete the Scavenger Hunt in one day!

* Waiting in line

Don't waste time in lines. If the wait is longer than 15 minutes, use Genie+ on your phone's Disneyland app (if Genie+ is available and you feel like coughing up the $), move on to the next attraction, and come back during your Genie+ time window. Exception: In some attractions, the Hidden Mickey(s) can only be seen from the Standby (regular) queue line, and not from the Lightning Lane. (I've not suggested Genie+ in the Clues section when that is the case.) The lines at the most popular attractions should not be too long if you start your scavenger hunt when the park opens and follow the hunt Clues as given. If you do encounter long lines, another option is to return later during a parade or in the hour before the park closes. Alternatively, if you need to board an attraction with a long wait without Genie+, use the Single Rider queue if available. (Check your Guidemap for a big "S" symbol next to the attractions with Single Rider queues.)

* Playing fair

Be considerate of other guests. Some Hidden Mickeys are in restaurants and shops. Ask a Cast Member's permission before searching inside sit-down restaurants and avoid the busy mealtime hours unless you're one of the diners. Tell the Cast Members and other guests who see you looking around what you're up to, so they can share in the fun.

Finding Hidden Mickeys Without Scavenger Hunting

If scavenger hunts don't appeal to you, you don't have to use them. You can find Hidden Mickeys in the specific rides and other attractions you visit by using the Index to Mickey's Hiding Places in the back of this book. Look up the attraction, restaurant, hotel, or shop in the Index, turn to the appropriate page in the book, and then follow the Clue(s) to find the Hidden Mickey(s).

- Caution: You won't find every attraction, restaurant, hotel, or shop in the Index. Only those with confirmed Hidden Mickeys are included in this guide.

Hidden Mickeys: Real or Wishful Thinking?

The classic (three-circle) Mickeys are the most controversial—for good reason. Much debate surrounds the gathering of circular forms throughout Disneyland. The three cannonball craters in the wall of the fort in *Pi-*

rates of the Caribbean (Clue 35 in the Disneyland Park Scavenger Hunt) is obviously the work of a clever artist. However, three-circle configurations occur spontaneously in art and nature, as in collections of grapes, tomatoes, pumpkins, bubbles, oranges, cannonballs, and the like. Unlike the cannonball crater Hidden Mickey in *Pirates of the Caribbean*, it may be difficult to attribute a random "classic Mickey" configuration of circles to a deliberate lmagineer design.

So which groupings of three circles qualify as Hidden Mickeys as opposed to wishful thinking? Unfortunately, no master list of actual or "lmagineer-approved" Hidden Mickeys exists. Purists demand that a true classic Hidden Mickey should have proper proportions and positioning. The round head must be larger than the ear circles (so that three equal circles in the proper alignment would not qualify as a Hidden Mickey). The head and ears must be touching and in perfect position for Mickey's head and ears.

On the other hand, Disney's mantra is: "If the guest thinks it's a Hidden Mickey, then by golly it is one!" Of course, I appreciate Disney's respect for their guests' opinions. However, when the subject is Hidden Mickeys, let's apply some guidelines. My own criteria are looser than the purist's but stricter than the "anything goes" Disney approach. I prefer to use a few sensible guidelines.

To be classified as a genuine classic Hidden Mickey, the three circles should satisfy the following criteria:

1. Purposeful (sometimes you can sense that the circles were placed on purpose).

2. Proportionate sizes (head larger than the ears and somewhat proportionate to the ears).

3. Round or at least "roundish."

4. The ears don't touch each other, and the ears are above the head (not beside it).

5. The head and ears touch or they're close to touching.

6. The grouping of circles is exceptional or unique in appearance.

7. The circles are hidden or somewhat hidden and not obviously decor (decorative).

Having spelled out some ground rules, allow me now to bend them in one instance. Some Hidden Mickeys are sentimental favorites with Disney fans, even though they may actually represent "wishful thinking." (My neighbor, Lew Brooks, calls them "two-beer" Mickeys.) Who am I to defy tradition? For example, the three circles on the back of the turtle in *Snow White's Enchanted Wish* (Clue 102 in the Disneyland Park Scavenger Hunt) form a not-quite-proportionate "classic" Mickey. However, if you ask Cast Members near this attraction about a Hidden Mickey, they may whisper to you these cryptic words: "Watch for the turtle!"

Hidden Mickeys vs. Decorative Mickeys

Some Mickeys are truly hidden, not visible to the guest. They may be located behind the scenes, available only to Cast Members. You won't find them in this field guide, as I only include Hidden Mickeys that are accessible to the guest. Other Mickeys are decorative; they were placed in plain sight to enhance the decor. For example, in a restaurant, I consider a pat of butter shaped like Mickey Mouse to be a decorative (aka decor) Mickey. Disneyland is loaded with decorative Mickeys. You'll find obvious images of Mickey Mouse on items such as manhole covers, displays in shop windows, and restaurant menus. I do not include these ubiquitous and sometimes changing images in this book unless they are unique or hard to spot.

Hidden Mickeys can change or be accidentally (or purposefully) removed over time by the processes of nature or by the continual cleaning and refurbishing that goes on at Disneyland. For example, Clarabelle's Snack Stand with its classic Hidden Mickey on a shutter is no longer with us. Cast Members themselves sometimes create or remove Hidden Mickeys.

My Selection Process

I trust you've concluded by now that Hidden Mickey Science is an evolving specialty. Which raises the question: how did I choose the more than 415 Hidden Mickeys in the scavenger hunts in this guide? I compiled my list of Hidden Mickeys from all the resources to which I had access: my own sightings, images sent to me by others (see "Acknowledgements," page 153), websites, books, and Cast Members. (Cast Members in each specific area usually—but not always!—know where some Hidden Mickeys are located.) Then I embarked on my verification hunts, asking for help along the way from generous Disney Cast Members. I have included only those Hidden Mickeys I could personally verify.

Furthermore, some Hidden Mickeys are visible only intermittently or only from certain vantage points in ride vehicles. I don't generally include these Mickeys, unless I feel that adequate descriptions will allow anyone to find them. So, the scavenger hunts include only those images I believe to be recognizable as Hidden Mickeys and visible to the general touring guest. It is quite likely, though, that one or more of the Hidden Mickeys described in this book will disappear over time.

Take note: on the following pages, the newest (to the book) Hidden Mickeys are underlined!

If you find one missing before I do, I hope you'll let me know by sending a message to my website:

www.HiddenMickeyguy.com

I have enjoyed finding each and every Hidden Mickey in this book. I'm certain I'll find more as time goes by, and I hope you can spot new Hidden Mickeys during your visit. So, put on some comfortable walking shoes and experience the Disneyland Resort like you never have before! Enjoy the Hunt!

- Steve Barrett

Notes

Chapter 2

Disneyland Park Scavenger Hunt

*
Arrive at the entrance turnstiles (with your admission ticket) 45 minutes before the opening time for early entry (if you're eligible) or 45 minutes before official opening time if it's a non-early entry day.

Note: If Disneyland is crowded, it's more feasible to spread the Hidden Mickeys Scavenger Hunt over two days.

*
If you want to spend the extra cash, pay for the current version of *Disney Genie+* and/or *Individual Lightning Lane* (you'll pay a separate cost for each one) to enter your chosen attraction's Lightning Lane and accelerate your hunts in the parks. You can access these extra services on the *Disneyland* app (it's free to download) on your smart phone. On certain attractions, however, Hidden Mickeys can only be seen from the Standby (regular) queue. You'll miss them if you take the Lightning Lane route. Therefore, to speed up your hunts even more (if you choose to spend the money), I recommend reserving Lightning Lane (by purchasing the current version of *Disney Genie+*) for one or more of the following:

- *Matterhorn Bobsleds, Space Mountain, Haunted Mansion, Indiana Jones Adventure, Big Thunder Mountain Railroad*, and/or *"it's a small world"*.

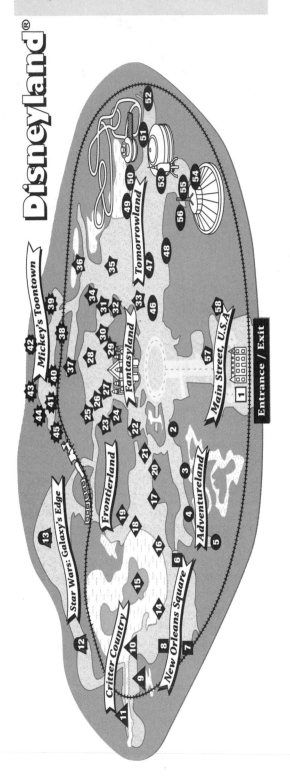

22

Disneyland®

1. Disneyland® Railroad, Entrance

Adventureland
2. Walt Disney's Enchanted Tiki Room
3. Jungle Cruise
4. Adventureland Treehouse
5. Indiana Jones™ Adventure

New Orleans Square
6. Pirates of the Caribbean
7. Disneyland® Railroad
8. Haunted Mansion

Critter Country
9. Bayou Adventure
10. Davy Crockett's Explorer Canoes
11. The Many Adventures of Winnie the Pooh

Star Wars: Galaxy's Edge
12. Star Wars: Rise of the Resistance
13. Millennium Falcon: Smugglers Run

Frontierland
14. Raft to Tom Sawyer Island
15. Pirates Lair on Tom Sawyer Island
16. Fantasmic!
17. The Golden Horseshoe Stage
18. Mark Twain Riverboat and Sailing Ship Columbia
19. Big Thunder Mountain Railroad
20. Pioneer Mercantile shop
21. Frontierland Shootin' Exposition

Fantasyland
22. Fantasy Faire
23. Pinocchio's Daring Journey
24.
25. Casey Jr. Circus Train
26. King Arthur Carrousel
27. Sleeping Beauty Castle Walkthrough
28. Dumbo the Flying Elephant
29. Peter Pan's Flight
30. Mr. Toad's Wild Ride
31. Mad Tea Party
32. Alice in Wonderland
33. Pixie Hollow
34. Storybook Land Canal Boats
35. Matterhorn Bobsleds
36. "it's a small world"
37. Fantasyland Theatre

Mickey's Toontown
38. Disneyland® Railroad
39. Roger Rabbit's Car Toon Spin
40. Goofy's
41. Donald's Duck Pond
42. Mickey & Minnie's Runaway Railway
43. Minnie's House
44. Mickey's House
45. Chip 'n' Dale's GADGETcoaster

Tomorrowland
46. Astro Orbitor
47. Buzz Lightyear Astro Blasters
48. Star Tours - The Adventures Continue
49. Finding Nemo Submarine Voyage
50. Disneyland® Monorail
51. Autopia
52. Disneyland® Railroad
53. Star Wars Launch Bay
54. Space Mountain
55. Tomorrowland Theater
56. Starcade

Main Street, U.S.A.
57. Main Street Cinema
58. The Disneyland® Story … Mr. Lincoln

Fit your Lightning Lane choice(s) any-where in my Scavenger Hunt plan. If you don't opt for the Lightning Lane options, just follow my Scavenger Hunt plan for efficient touring.

Clue 1: As soon as you pass through the entrance turnstiles, look around for a classic Mickey.
3 points

*Whenever you find yourself on Main Street, U.S.A., keep an eye out for the **Fire Engine** or a **Horseless Carriage vehicle.**

Clue 2: Check near the driver for a Hidden Mickey or Minnie.
3 bonus points

*If it's an early-entry day, ride *Peter Pan's Flight, Mr. Toad's Wild Ride,* and *Alice in Wonderland* and then walk to Star Wars: Galaxy's Edge and enter the Standby queue for *Millennium Falcon: Smugglers Run.*

If it's a non-early entry day, start with *Peter Pan's Flight* and proceed with the Hunt!

*Ride **Peter Pan's Flight**
Clue 3: Study the handrail posts near the loading dock for a Hidden Mickey.
4 points

Clue 4: At the beginning of the ride, read two names in blocks below you.
4 points for finding both

Clue 5: Look for Mickey in Big Ben.
5 points

Clue 6: <u>Don't miss a Hidden Mickey on the ship near Mr. Smee!</u>
5 points

24

*
Outside *Peter Pan's Flight* ...

Clue 7: Search high for a Hidden Mickey in a window.
3 points

*
Then walk toward the **Matter-horn Bobsleds**. Observe the side of the mountain that faces *"it's a small world."*

Clue 8: Locate a Mickey clearing in the snow.
5 points

*
Line up for the Bobsleds ride in the right hand queue.

Clue 9: Study the right Bobsleds queue area for a Hidden Mickey on a coat of arms.
4 points

Clue 10: While on the ride, stay alert for a Hidden Mickey in an ice cave.
5 bonus points

Clue 11: Walk to a small alcove near the exit of the *Matterhorn Bobsleds* and find Nemo!
4 points

*
Walk to Adventureland and enjoy **Indiana Jones™ Adventure**.

Clue 12: Stay alert for a Hidden Mickey made of pearls on the wall of the inside queue.
4 points

Clue 13: Study the walls of the stand-by queue for Mickey's "initials."
4 points

Clue 14: In the circular room with the rope you can pull on, search for a

stone slab (propped upright) with a tiny classic Mickey. (Note: This image is becoming more faint with time and may disappear.)
5 points

Clue 15: Now look up for another classic Mickey in the same room.
3 points

Clue 16: Find a large classic Mickey in the room with the video screen.
3 points

Clue 17: Toward the end of the video room, look up and say "hi" to Eeyore!
4 points

Clue 18: When you leave the video room, peer into an office to spot Mickey (and/or Minnie).
3 points

Clue 19: After the ride starts, gaze up into Mara's huge face for a classic Mickey.
3 points

Clue 20: When your vehicle enters the Mummy Room, find a Mickey hat!
5 points

* Now hop on *Jungle Cruise*.

Clue 21: Glance up outside the entrance for a Hidden Character.
2 points

Clue 22: In the last part of the entrance queue, stay vigilant for a Hidden Mickey inside a bag in a caged display. It's best seen from the right-side queue.
3 points

Clue 23: On the boat ride, check out the gorilla camp scene for a Hidden Mickey on the ground.
4 points

* Turn left at the exit to enjoy **Haunted Mansion**.

Clue 24: Look high along the mansion walls inside for a Hidden Mickey.
3 points

Clue 25: Search for Mickey in the wallpaper.
3 points

Clue 26: While on the ride, can you find Donald Duck?
4 points

Clue 27: Study a floating table for a Hidden Mickey.
4 points

Clue 28: If snow is in the ballroom, find Mickey!
5 points

Clue 29: As you ride, keep alert for plates and saucers.
3 points

Clue 30: In the attic, look for a clock with a Hidden Mickey.
5 points

* Hop on **Pirates of the Caribbean**.

Clue 31: During the first part of your boat ride, study the water for Mickey.
5 points

Clue 32: Stay alert for Mickey on a chair by a bed.
4 points

Clue 33: After you pass the skeleton in bed, look back for an image of Goofy.
5 points

Clue 34: In the first fight scene with the pirate ship firing cannonballs, watch a window in a building for Mickey.
5 points

Clue 35: In the first fight scene, spot a classic Mickey on a wall.
5 points

Clue 36: Stare at the wall behind the cats by the drunken pirate. See a classic Mickey?
4 points

Clue 37: Near the end of the ride, study the armor on the wall for a classic Mickey.
5 points

Clue 38: Find a classic Mickey on a chair in Jack Sparrow's treasure room.
4 points

Clue 39: After you exit the boat, look around for a classic Mickey on a door.
2 points

Clue 40: Study the outside railings in New Orleans Square for some famous initials (another Hidden Surprise).
5 points for both names

*Walk to *Big Thunder Mountain Railroad* in Frontierland.

Clue 41: Look for a Hidden Mickey on a sign outside the attraction.
4 points

Clue 42: While on the ride, search for three gears that form a classic Mickey.
3 points

Clue 43: Find Mickey at the exit.
3 points

*
Ride ***Millennium Falcon: Smugglers Run***

Clue 44: <u>Along the inside Standby entrance queue, stay alert for a coiled cable Hidden Mickey.</u>
3 points

Clue 45: Look around the briefing room (just before you enter the cockpit) for a classic Hidden Mickey.
3 points

Clue 46: When you're seated in the cockpit, search the ceiling for a Hidden Mickey.
3 points

Clue 47: Stroll around the area near the entrance to *Millennium Falcon Smuggler's Run* for a Hidden Mickey on an outside wall.
4 points

Clue 48: <u>Check out the Market restaurants and shops. Study the wall above the entrance to the restrooms for an upside-down classic Hidden Mickey.</u>
4 points

Clue 49: Explore the middle entrance to Star Wars: Galaxy's Edge (the entrance across from *Big Thunder Mountain Railroad*) and search a rock wall near the bridge for a Hidden Mickey.
5 points

Clue 50: While you're near the bridge at this middle entrance, look up for a rock shaped like Donald Duck.
4 points

*When you're ready for lunch, mosey on over to **The Golden Horseshoe** in Frontierland for a decent counter-service meal.

Clue 51: Check around the stage for a classic Mickey.
3 points

Clue 52: Now study the wall paintings for a Hidden Mickey.
3 points

*Walk to *Mickey's Toontown*.
(Note: You'll find many Mickey shapes throughout Toontown. I don't include the larger, more obvious Mickey images as Hidden Mickeys; they're more properly designated decor Mickeys.)

*Mosey to **Mickey & Minnie's Runaway Railway**. (All new Hidden Mickeys!)

Clue 53: Enjoy Hidden Mickeys in a corner of the cartoon posters on the walls of the inside queue.
2 points

Clue 54: Search for one of these cartoon posters with a pink paint classic Mickey.
4 points

Clue 55: Along the Standby queue, stay alert for a cord on the floor which is looped into a Hidden Mickey.
3 points

Clue 56: When the pre-show cartoon video begins, don't miss the Hidden Mickey on Mickey's car.
3 points

Clue 57: On the ride, in the Carnival Room, spot a classic Mickey made of rolls of admission tickets.
3 points

Clue 58: Also in the Carnival Room, check out the classic Hidden Mickey in the 'Frontier Toss' game.
4 points

Clue 59: As you're floating fast toward the waterfall, scan left for Mickey in a tree.
4 points

Clue 60: At the bottom of the waterfall, focus on a large clam in the middle for a (split-second) classic Hidden Mickey.
5 points

Clue 61: As you enter the room with the city scene, look up for a classic Hidden Mickey on a billboard.
5 points

Clue 62: Spot an ice cream Hidden Mickey to your right.
3 points

Clue 63: Squint for Mickey Mouse on a clothesline above Donald Duck's delivery truck.
5 points

Clue 64: In Daisy Duck's dance class room, check out classic Hidden Mickeys on the lower wall.
3 points

Clue 65: Study the large moving flowers for a Hidden Mickey!
4 points

Clue 66: While leaving the dance class room, enjoy moving light Hidden Mickeys.
3 points

Clue 67: In the Factory Room, notice a small yellow upright classic Mickey to your right.
3 points

Clue 68: In the last room, scan the low blue wall on the left side of the railroad track for a familiar name.
5 points

Clue 69: In the last room, marvel at fireworks Hidden Mickeys.
2 points

Clue 70: After you leave your ride vehicle, stay alert for Hidden Mickeys on the walls in front of and behind you.
2 points

* Get in line for **Chip 'n' Dale's GADGETcoaster**. The Hidden Mickeys here are along the queue. You can skip the actual ride if you want; just ask to exit when you reach the loading area.

Clue 71: Stay alert for at least three rock classic Mickeys in the queue walls.
3 points each; 9 points total

Clue 72: Gaze around the vehicle loading area for a Hidden Mickey.
4 points

* Stroll over to **Mickey's House**.

Clue 73: See anything in his front door?
1 point

Clue 74: Glance down for Mickey.
1 point

Clues 75 and 76: Look inside a glass-fronted bookcase for some Hidden Mickeys.
3 points total for finding one on each of two books

Clue 77: Stare at other books in the first room.
3 points

Clues 78 and 79: In the piano room, search for two Hidden Mickeys in a bookcase.
2 points each; 4 points total

Clue 80: <u>Find classic Mickeys and two other Hidden Characters in the piano.</u>
5 points for a Hidden Mickey and 2 other characters

Clue 81: Something's atop the piano.
2 points

Clue 82: <u>In the piano room, don't miss one more book Hidden Mickey.</u>
2 points

Clue 83: Look for Mickey on a drum.
2 points

Clue 84: Spot Mickey on a clock.
2 points

Clue 85: Pay attention to a special mirror inside *Mickey's Movie Barn* (the room in Mickey's House where you wait to meet Mickey in person).
4 points

Clue 86: Study Donald's workbench for a paint-splotch Hidden Mickey.
3 points

Clue 87: Also, in *Mickey's Movie Barn*, watch the countdown screen.
3 points

Clue 88: Once outside, admire Mickey's car and find Hidden Mickeys.
3 points for one or more

* Saunter over to **Minnie's House**.

Clue 89: Mickey is hiding in Minnie's kitchen.
2 points

Now search for Mickey outside Minnie's House.

Clue 90: Look near and to the right of the big blue doors for a classic Hidden Mickey.
3 points

* Find the **Toontown Post Office**
Clue 91: Find two Hidden Mickeys and a few other Disney Characters.
4 points

* Clue 92: Ring the doorbell at the **Toontown Fire Department** and watch for a Hidden Mickey.
4 points

* Clue 93: <u>Check out the front doorknob of the **Toontown Insurance Company**. Remind you of anything?</u>
4 points

* Queue up to ride **Alice in Wonderland**.

Clue 94: In the first part of the ride, watch for a small house (the White Rabbit's house) for a Hidden Mickey inside the open window.
5 points

Clue 95: <u>Now stare to your left for two mushrooms, each with a Hidden Mickey.</u>
5 points for both

Clue 96: On the ride, search for a classic Mickey in red paint.
4 points

* Get in line for **Mr. Toad's Wild Ride**.
Clue 97: Find a tiny Mickey along the inside entrance queue.
4 points

Clue 98: At the beginning of the ride, stare at a right-hand door for a tiny dark Mickey in the door's stained glass.
5 points

Clue 99: Search for Mickey in beer foam.
4 points

Clue 100: Stay alert for Sherlock Holmes in a window. (A Hidden Surprise, not a Hidden Mickey!)
5 points

*
Step over to **Snow White 's Enchanted Wish**.

Clue 101: Find Mickey at the loading dock.
3 points

Clue 102: On the ride, watch for a classic Mickey on an animal.
3 points

Clue 103: Check out a Hidden Tinker Bell near a mine car full of jewels on your left.
5 points

*
Go to **Pinocchio's Daring Journey** in Fantasyland.

Clue 104: <u>Search a loading dock mural for a Pleasure Island Hidden Mickey.</u>
3 points

Clue 105: Scan the loading dock area for a Hidden Mickey in front of a blue door.
3 points

Clue 106: Watch the floor to spot a yellow Hidden Mickey.
4 points

Clue 107: Check the popcorn stand on your right for a classic Mickey.
4 points

Clue 108: Spot a Hidden Mickey under a glass globe with a fish.
4 points

Clue 109: Look for a Hidden Mickey near a ship.
5 points

*Walk to the **Storybook Land Canal Boats** ride and study the boats before you board and after you exit your boat.

Clue 110: A Hidden Mickey is on the back of the "Daisy" boat.
3 points

Clue 111: Don't forget the "Wendy" boat's Hidden Mickey!
2 points

Clue 112: On the boat ride, squint for a tiny classic Mickey on a rear building in Pinocchio's Village, just after Monstro the Whale.
5 points

Clue 113: While on the boat ride, search for a Hidden Mickey near Cinderella's village.
3 points

*Make time in your schedule for the **afternoon parade**. (Note: The parade floats change from time to time but usually include Hidden Mickeys in their decoration.) The antique Grand Marshal automobile sometimes leads the parade.
Clue 114: Search this antique car for several Hidden Mickeys.
5 bonus points for finding three or more

*
Ride *Mark Twain Riverboat* or
Sailing Ship Columbia.

Clue 115: Study a bridge for a classic
Hidden Mickey washer under a bolt.
5 points

Clue 116: Squint for a Hidden Mickey
hole under the bridge.
5 points

Clue 117: Seek out the *Mark Twain
Riverboat* (if you haven't already). Concentrate on the front of the ship to spot
Hidden Mickeys.
2 points

Clue 118: Search for Mickey Mouse in a
painting near the *Mark Twain Riverboat* loading dock.
5 points

*
Float on the Raft to *Tom Sawyer
Island*.

Clue 119: On *Tom Sawyer Island*, seek
out a cavern entrance with a classic
Mickey.
3 points

Clue 120: Look for two Hidden Mickey
locks in a cave.
3 points

Clue 121: Study the treasure in the *Pirate's Lair* for a classic Mickey.
4 points

*
Relax on a gentle boat ride at *"it's a
small world."*

Clue 122: Look for Mickey along the
entrance queue.
3 points

Clue 123: Stay alert for Hidden Characters.
5 points for spotting five or more

Clue 124: Study a balloon above you for a Hidden Mickey bear shadow.
4 points

Clue 125: Keep your eyes peeled for a bear's head that looks like Mickey's head.
3 points

Clue 126: Near the end of the ride, watch the ceiling for a Hidden Mickey.
4 points

* Hop on the **Disneyland® Railroad** train at the Mickey's Toontown station. You can exit at Tomorrowland station and walk to your next destination.

Clue 127: Now keep your eyes peeled for a Hidden Mickey in grapes.
3 points

* Head next to **Buzz Lightyear Astro Blasters** in Tomorrowland.

Clue 128: Find two classic (three-circle) Hidden Mickeys along the entrance queue.
6 points for finding both

Clue 129: Search for two Mickey continents along the entrance queue.
6 points for finding both

Clue 130: Now spot an oblong satellite on the wall with a Hidden Mickey on its side.
4 points

Clue 131: On the ride, watch to your left for a classic Mickey on a block.
3 points

Clue 132: After you step off the ride vehicle, search for a side-profile Mickey on the wall.
2 points

Clue 133: Find two classic Mickeys in the same area.
2 points each

* Check into **Star Tours-The Adventures Continue**.

Clue 134: Along the entrance queue, spot a Hidden Mickey near C-3PO.
3 points

Clue 135: Now wait for a shadow Hidden Mickey in a video on a wall display along the entrance queue.
4 points

Clue 136: Next, study the entrance queue luggage scanner for Mickey and other Disney characters and images.
5 points total for finding Mickey and two or more other Disney images

Clue 137: After you're seated in the ride vehicle, C-3PO appears on a screen to your right. Scan him for Mickey!
5 points

Clue 138: At the end of the ride, if you dive down to the Coruscant planet (as opposed to other random end destinations for the ride), don't miss three faint blue circles that form a large classic Mickey on the right side of the screen.
5 bonus points

Clue 139: As your vehicle continues down to Coruscant and crash lands on a platform, look for classic Mickeys on a rear wall.
5 bonus points

*
 Go to **Space Mountain** and walk
up the Standby entrance queue (or the
Single Rider queue). You can skip the
ride if you want; there were no Hidden
Mickeys in it last time I checked.

Clue 140: See anything on the ride
vehicles?
2 points

*
 Walk to Tomorrowland. Go to **Finding Nemo Submarine Voyage** and
then look for the *Monorail* exit to find
the elevator for the **Disneyland®
Monorail**.

Clue 141: First go up to the *Monorail*
exit deck to spot a Hidden Mickey near
the water below you. (Note: This Hidden Mickey comes and goes.)
4 bonus points

Clue 142: Now search for Mickey near
the elevator on the ground level.
5 points

Ask a Cast Member for permission to
enter the **Marine Observation Outpost** at the right side of the *Finding
Nemo Submarine Voyage* entrance
queue.

Clue 143: Look around inside for a Hidden Mickey.
4 points

*
 Walk along the entrance queue for
Autopia.
Clue 144: Find a classic Mickey on the
cars.
3 points

Clue 145: Stroll toward Fantasyland
and search for a Mickey-shaped hole on
the outside of Matterhorn Mountain.
4 points

40

* Line up at the **Pixie Hollow** meet and greet area.

Clue 146: Near the end of the waiting queue, don't overlook a classic Mickey.
4 points

* Now walk to **The Many Adventures of Winnie the Pooh** in Critter Country.

Clue 147: Study the "Hunny Pot" vehicles for a classic Mickey.
2 points

Clue 148: Just after the ride starts, be aware of a classic Mickey in the wood.
5 points

Clue 149: After the Heffalumps and Woozles dream room, search high behind you for a Hidden Surprise. (It's not a Hidden Mickey, but it's a cool image that everyone should enjoy.)
5 points

Clue 150: Look for classic Mickey circles near Heffalumps.
3 points

Visit **Pooh Corner** store nearby.

Clue 151: Discover a Hidden Surprise inside the store: two references to the Country Bear Jamboree - a previous attraction near this site.
4 points

Walk to the **Briar Patch** store (near *Bayou Adventure*).

Clue 152: Look inside the store for a Hidden Mickey on a shelf.
3 points

* Stroll toward **Walt Disney's Enchanted Tiki Room**.

Clue 153: Observe the shields outside near the exit to find a classic Mickey.
3 points

* Stop in at the **Frontierland Shootin' Exposition**.

Clue 154: Spot a Hidden Mickey toward the front of the shootin' area.
3 points

* Enter the **Pioneer Mercantile** shop.

Clue 155: Examine the wall for Mickey.
3 points

* Walk to the **Rancho del Zocalo Restaurante**. Consider having dinner here or a bit later in this Hunt at the Plaza Inn Restaurant.

Clue 156: Search inside the restaurant for a classic Mickey in wood.
4 points

* Cross to the front of Frontierland, facing the central hub.

Clue 157: Look for a Hidden Mickey along the entrance walkway to Frontierland.
3 points

* Walk to **Fantasy Faire**.
Clue 158: Search for a classic Hidden Mickey inside the Music Box.
5 points

Clue 159: Now scan the crowd inside the Music Box for Disney Characters.
5 points for five or more

*
Stroll over to **King Arthur Carrousel**. Find the Hidden Mickeys from outside the carrousel.

Clue 160: Check out a horse in the outer circle for Hidden Mickeys.
2 points each; 4 points total

*
Cross Fantasyland to the **Mad Hatter shop**, not far from the *Mad Tea Party* attraction.

Clue 161: Search around inside the shop for a Hidden cat.
5 points

Clue 162: Spot Hidden Mickeys outside the shop.
2 points each for two Hidden Mickeys

*
Retrace your steps to **The Star Trader** shop (not far from *Star Tours*).

Clue 163: Glance inside *The Star Trader* for small classic Mickeys in poles. (You can spot this image in other Disney stores as well).
2 points

Clue 164: Now find two different Hidden Mickeys on merchandise bins. (You can spot these images in other Disney stores as well).
3 points for finding both types

*
Step over to the **Little Green Men Store Command** (next to *Buzz Lightyear Astro Blasters*).

Clue 165: Look for Mickey on a sign.
4 points

*Walk toward the central hub.

Clue 166: Study the spheres of the **Astro Orbitor**.
2 points

*Return to Main Street, U.S.A.

Clue 167: Check a painting inside the **Plaza Inn Restaurant**.
3 points

*Stand outside the **Silhouette Studio**.

Clue 168: Spot a Hidden Mickey in a display window.
4 points

Clue 169: Find a Hidden Mickey outside on a **fruit cart**.
4 points

*Stroll down Main Street to **Main Street Cinema**. Walk inside.

Clue 170: Look around for some Hidden Mickeys.
3 points for one or more

Clue 171: Outside *Main Street Cinema*, search for two Hidden Mickeys.
2 points each; 4 points total

*Find more Mickeys at the **Main Street Magic Shop**.

Clue 172: Spot Mickey on a display shelf.
3 points

Clue 173: Now look up for Mickey!
4 points

Clue 174: Locate a classic Mickey outside the shop.
3 points

* Stroll toward the Castle to the **Jolly Holiday Bakery Cafe.**

Clue 175: <u>Inside the Cafe, near one of the exit doors, look up for a Hidden Mickey made of lights.</u>
3 points

* Walk to the **Penny Arcade**.

Clue 176: Don't miss the small Hidden Mickey on a game machine inside the *Penny Arcade*!
4 points

* Approach the **Gibson Girl Ice Cream Parlor**.

Clue 177: Admire the outside windows for a Hidden Mickey.
4 points

* Stroll to the **Emporium** store.

Clue 178: Inside an entrance at the end of the store closest to *City Hall*, search for Mickey in a painting on the wall.
5 points

Clue 179: Find a room in the store with toy merchandise and look for a train circling a track overhead. Wait for a lighted Hidden Mickey to appear!
5 points

* Cross Main Street to the **Mad Hatter**.

Clue 180: Scan all the windows outside the store for a Hidden Mickey.
5 points

* Walk to the Main Street Station of the *Disneyland® Railroad*.

Clue 181: Wait for the trains and study their forward sections for Hidden Mickeys.
5 points total for one or more

* Watch the *Fantasmic!* show for Hidden Mickeys.

Clue 182: Be alert for a Hidden Mickey in white foam on the water screen.
5 points

Clue 183: Study a mirror for a Hidden Mickey.
4 points

* Don't miss the nighttime *fireworks* show!

Clue 184: Watch the sky during the fireworks show for a Hidden Mickey.
5 bonus points

* Exit Disneyland Park®.
Clue 185: In the *entrance plaza*, look for Mickey at your feet.
3 points

Clue 186: Spot Mickey at the tops and bottoms of some of the poles.
4 points for spotting Mickey in both places

Now total your score and see how you did.

Total Points for Disneyland Park =

How'd You Do?

Up to 265 points - Bronze
266 to 529 points - Silver
530 points and over - Gold
663 points - Perfect Score

(If you earned bonus points by spotting
Hidden Mickeys in the *Main Street Fire
Engine* or *Horseless Carriage vehicle*, the
Matterhorn Bobsleds' ice cave, *Star Tours*,
the boat docks at *Finding Nemo Submarine Voyage*, on the Grand Marshal's car
during the *afternoon parade*, or during
the evening *fireworks* show, you may have
done even better.)

If you need help, the Hints are here for you!

Entrance

Hint 1: As soon as you enter Disneyland, turn around and spot the classic Mickey speaker grid on the utility box next to the entrance turnstile. (Note: The ticket attendant may be blocking your view.)

Hint 2: Whenever you walk along Main Street, U.S.A., look for the *Fire Engine* or a *Horseless Carriage vehicle*. In front of the driver, the key chain hanging from the ignition key often holds a smiling Mickey Mouse or Minnie Mouse.

49

Fantasyland

- Peter Pan's Flight

Hint 3: When you reach the section of the entrance queue that's alongside the loading dock area, find the seventh handrail post from the end of the handrail to your right. Midway up the post, an upright classic Hidden Mickey design faces you.

Hint 4: As you walk through the entrance queue, lean over the rail and look into the first scene (the bedroom) of the ride. Alphabet blocks are stacked and scattered on the floor. On the ride, as your vehicle soars over the bedroom, look down at the blocks and find these words: "PETER PAN" and then "DISNEY" (spelled as "D1XNEY"). (Cast Members sometimes change these blocks around.)

Hint 5: As you soar over London, a side-view Mickey silhouette hides in a top window on the far side of Big Ben. Look back at the window as you fly around the clock tower.

Hint 6: While soaring over the ship where Peter Pan is sword-fighting with Captain Hook, spot the cannonballs that form an upside-down classic Mickey against a red post and behind Mr. Smee.

Hint 7: Inside a high window to the left of the entrance to the attraction, sideways classic Mickeys are on the bottom of a plush bear's (or lion's) paw. The paw is at the lower right of the leftmost window, next to the window curtain.

- *Matterhorn Bobsleds*

Hint 8: Admire the Matterhorn from in front of Le Petit Chalet shop near *"it's a small world."* About two-thirds the way up the side of the mountain, a clearing in the snow forms a classic Mickey, tilted to the left.

Hint 9: A tiny black classic Mickey is in the middle of a red and white coat of arms at the rear of the right queue. The Mickey is on a red triangle at the bottom of a white pole.

Hint 10: To your left during the first part of the ride, on the floor of the first ice cave, where you will see expedition equipment and glowing crystals, a rope between the ice crystals and the crates is coiled into a classic Mickey. (Note: This Hidden Mickey comes and goes.)

Hint 11: Now for a Hidden Surprise! Exit *Matterhorn Bobsleds* on the Tomorrow-land side to find a Hidden Nemo (which is fading with time) traced on the side of a wooden electrical box. It's across the walkway from the Matterhorn exit at an entrance to a small alcove.

Adventureland

- *Indiana Jones™ Adventure*

Hint 12: A full-body painting of Mara is on the wall to your right just as you enter the inside part of the queue. She is pouring coins, jewels, and pearls out of a bowl. An upside-down classic Mickey made of pearls is at the lower end of the long string of pearls.

Hint 13: Across from the first drinking fountains in the inside standby queue, Mickey's initials, "MM" in Mara script, are on the left wall, just above a horizontal crack in the wall.

Hint 14: On the side of a bamboo structure just opposite the hanging rope, a large painted stone slab has a tiny light blue classic Hidden Mickey symbol on the lower right edge of the circle of symbols around Mara's face. (Note: This image is becoming fainter with time and may disappear.)

Hint 15: On the ceiling, Mara's giant nose is a classic Mickey.

Hint 16: When you enter the room showing the video on a screen, study the left wall for a large classic Hidden Mickey between the last two lights on the wall.

Hint 17: *Indiana Jones™ Adventure* was built over a previous Eeyore (cast) parking lot. As a tribute to the past, an original white parking sign in the shape of Eeyore was placed in the video room, high up in the rafters. To spot this Hidden Surprise, go to the end of the video room, turn around, and look up to the left of the projector. If you can't find it, ask a nearby Cast Member for help.

Hint 18: In an office just past the video room, Mickey and Minnie Mouse are pictured on a partially visible magazine cover. The magazine is on a desktop. (Note: These magazine images are moved around and may not be visible at times.)

Hint 19: Shortly after the ride starts, look at Mara's face for a (not quite perfect) classic Mickey formed by the curves of the nostrils and the oval depression just below the middle of the nose.

Hint 20: As soon as your vehicle turns a corner and enters the Mummy Room, look left for a skeleton wearing a Mickey Mouse hat. Let's hope the hat stays put!

- Jungle Cruise

Hint 21: Beneath the outside *Jungle Cruise* sign, a mask that resembles Donald Duck hangs just above the entrance.

Hint 22: Along the entrance queue, inside a caged display entitled "Safari Staging Area," a bag with a camera and other provisions lies against the side of the display next to the part of the queue near the loading area. Three lenses on the camera form a classic Hidden Mickey.

Hint 23: At the front of the gorilla camp scene to the right of the boat, three pieces of dinnerware – a plate or pan for the "head" and two small round bowls for the "ears" – come together as a classic Mickey.

New Orleans Square
- Haunted Mansion

Hint 24: As soon as you walk through the front door along the entrance queue, go to any of the candlestick holders on the wall and, with your back to the wall, look up from underneath to spot a classic Mickey effect.

Hint 25: Large circles form classic Mickeys in the wallpaper of the Art Gallery after you exit the Stretching Room.

Hint 26: As you pass by the "endless hallway" in your Doom Buggy, check out the back of the purple chair for an abstract Donald Duck. Near the top of the chair, you can see his cap, which sits above his distorted eyes, face and bill. (Note: The chair location may change at times.)

Hint 27: In the Séance room, a floating table above you has a tilted classic Mickey design at the top of the legs and just below the tabletop.

Hint 28: In the Ballroom scene, "snow" may dust the floor at the right rear of the room. When it does, a classic Mickey formed of snow is usually somewhere in the snowdrift.

Hint 29: During the Ballroom scene, look down at the place settings near the center of the dining table. You'll see two small saucers and one larger plate forming a classic Mickey. The Cast Members move this Hidden Mickey around at times.

Hint 30: After the ballroom scene, look to the right as soon as you enter the attic. Find the clock on a bureau to the right of the oval portrait of a bride and groom and just to the right of a bright orange and blue lamp. A brown classic Mickey hides behind the pendulum of the clock.

- *Pirates of the Caribbean*

Hint 31: As you drift past the Blue Bayou Restaurant seating area, a classic Mickey appears in the water to the right of your boat. It's formed by the last set of three lily pads that you pass before you enter the caverns.

Hint 32: To the left of your boat, a classic Mickey hides on the upper back of the chair to the right of the bed where the pirate skeleton is lying.

Hint 33: Just after you float by the skeleton in bed on your left, look back at the ceiling of the cavern behind you for a large rock that juts out over the water above you. The shape of the rock resembles Goofy.

Hint 34: When you enter the battle scene with the pirate ship firing cannonballs, watch the window above and in front of you with the fighting silhouettes. At several points during the scuffle, you can spot an outline of Mickey's head and ears.

Hint 35: In the battle scene with the pirate ship firing cannonballs, there are three cannonball impact craters on the upper part of the fort wall on the right side of your boat. This crater classic Mickey is below the middle fort cannon and best seen if you turn around to view it as you are passing by the fort.

Hint 36: Stay alert for the cats to the right of the drunken pirate sitting on a barrel. A shadow on the wall behind the cats forms a classic Mickey at times.

Hint 37: This classic Mickey is to the left of your boat in the last room, where pieces of armor hang from the wall. Look for the gold breastplate, often the leftmost armor breastplate, with a coat of arms emblem. In the center of that emblem are classic Mickey circles. (Note: The items in the armor display are moved around at times.)

Hint 38: In the last treasure room to your left, three circles at the top of the back of Jack Sparrow's chair make a classic Mickey.

Hint 39: On the right side as you exit, and before you reach the street outside, a classic Mickey-shaped lock adorns a back door to the Pieces of Eight shop.

Hint 40: Out in New Orleans Square, a Hidden Surprise! Walt and Roy Disney's gold stylized initials are in the blue railing above the Royal Street Veranda.

Frontierland

- Big Thunder Mountain Railroad

Hint 41: An upside-down classic Hidden Mickey is formed of round rust or stain circles that surround bullet holes on the back of a wooden "Standby Entrance" sign in front of the attraction. The Mickey circles are next to an Ace of Clubs nailed to the back of the sign.

Hint 42: As you start to climb the second hill, look to your left, near the bottom of the hill, for three gears that form a large, upside-down classic Mickey.

Hint 43: On your right as you exit, several groups of green lobes in the cactus garden usually form classic Mickeys with oval heads and ears.

Star Wars: Galaxy's Edge

- Millennium Falcon: Smugglers Run

Hint 44: The inside Standby entrance queue loops around a large silver engine. On a metal platform below the engine, a cable is coiled into three circles that form a classic Hidden Mickey.

Hint 45: A sideways classic Hidden Mickey made of round silver metal wheels sits on one side of the wall video monitor.

Hint 46: On the middle front of the cockpit ceiling, a small metal classic Mickey is visible at times between two small flexible pipes, at the point where the pipes separate and angle away from each other.

- Elsewhere in Galaxy's Edge

Hint 47: On a wall near the entrance to *Millennium Falcon: Smugglers Run*, blast marks come together as a classic Hidden Mickey. To find the wall, go up the stairs or ramp to the left of the entrance to Millennium Falcon (as you face it). The Hidden Mickey is on a side wall, about five feet above the walkway.

Hint 48: Above the entrance to the restrooms in the Market, a large rectangular box is supported by struts on the wall. On the bottom of the box, to the right of the middle strut, is a small metal rectangle with circles and dials. Three circles (one large and two small) on the rectangle create an upside-down classic Hidden Mickey.

Hint 49: Walk from Frontierland along the middle entrance path to Star Wars: Galaxy's Edge. Pass under the bridge and scan the rock wall to your left. About 15 feet or so past the bridge, you'll spot a small, faint, dark classic Mickey marking a few inches above the walkway.

Hint 50: Now walk back toward the bridge and look up. A rock shaped like Donald Duck is perched next to and above the left side of the bridge. You'll see the side view of Donald's head silhouetted against the sky.

57

Frontierland
- *The Golden Horseshoe*

Hint 51: Walk toward the front of the stage and find a grate (or vent) in the center of the lower front wall. Start at the lower right hole in the grate. Then look up and diagonally left one hole to spot a classic Mickey image in the grating.

Hint 52: Look for the "Hall of Fame" picture on the left wall lower level. Sideways gold classic Mickeys hide at the middle sides of the frame around Betty Taylor's picture.

Mickey's Toontown

- *Mickey & Minnie's Runaway Railway* (All new Hidden Mickeys)

Hint 53: Along the walls of the inside queue, posters with titles of Disney cartoons show a small classic Mickey logo in each panel at the lower left corner.

Hint 54: In one of these posters, a pink paint classic Mickey is at the lower right side of the advertisement for the cartoon "Potatoland."

Hint 55: Along the Standby queue, in the center of a room, a long black coiled electrical cord is looped on the floor into a classic Hidden Mickey, which is below a red airplane and behind a book entitled "How to Fly."

Hint 56: In the pre-show cartoon video, the front of Mickey's car has a silver classic Mickey ornament.

Hint 57: On the ride, in the Carnival Room, a classic Hidden Mickey made of rolls of admission tickets is on a poster just to the left of Donald Duck, who is making a mess while preparing his hot dog.

Hint 58: Also in the Carnival Room, a classic Mickey (a bullseye 'head' and two blue 'ears') sits in the upper middle of the background of the 'Frontier Toss' game, which is on the left side of the room.

Hint 59: Along the ride, before the waterfall, look quickly to your left to spot a tree bending over the left side of the river. Three coconuts on the tree make a decent classic Mickey.

Hint 60: At the bottom of the waterfall, the large clam in the middle, turned slightly to the right, opens and shows three pearls in a classic Mickey formation, leaning to the left. The image appears for only a split second.

Hint 61: In the room with the city scene, look for three Hidden Mickeys: high on a rooftop straight in front of you, a white classic Mickey is on a bottle on a billboard advertising 'Delux-O-Detergent.'

Hint 62: #2 - a large classic Mickey is formed by ice cream scoops, tilted left, in a cone at the right side of the room.

Hint 63: #3 - in a recess in shadows at the left side of the city scene, a T-shirt with a full-body Mickey Mouse hangs high on the left side of a clothesline, to the left of a window in a building and just above Donald Duck's purple delivery truck.

Hint 64: In Daisy Duck's dance class room, sideways classic Hidden Mickeys are repeated in the design along the lower walls.

Hint 65: Watch for large moving flowers on the mirrors. A classic Hidden Mickey is in the center of one of the flowers on the right side.

Hint 66: While leaving Daisy Duck's dance room (and en route to the 'Factory Room'), watch the walls in and after the dance room for moving white light classic Mickeys.

Hint 67: In the 'Factory Room': a yellow upright classic Mickey on a red background is at the mid-right side of the room.

Hint 68: In the last room, as you approach the last part of the low blue wall on your left, "M-I-C-K-E-Y" is spelled in white elongated letters on the wall.

Hint 69: In the last room, listen for fireworks. On the left-side wall some of the fireworks come together to form classic Mickeys.

Hint 70: As you exit, a large classic Hidden Mickey made of film reels is on the wall in front of you, and a classic Hidden Mickey is in the lower left logo on the wall behind you.

- Chip 'n' Dale's GADGETcoaster

Hint 71: The following three classic Mickeys aren't perfectly proportional, but they seem purposeful:
  - The first is at the first turn to the left, on the right-side wall, in the entrance queue.
  - The second is on the right-side wall at the second right turn.
  - The third is a somewhat distorted classic Mickey, tilted sideways, at the end of the main wall on the left and about 20 feet before the boarding area.

Hint 72: Inside the loading area, turn around and locate the only blueprint on the rear wall. A partially hidden drawing of Mickey Mouse is on the right side of the blueprint. Under Mickey are the words "DOG & PONY FOR MICKEY AT 4 PM."

- *Approaching, in, and exiting Mickey's House*

Hint 73: The window in Mickey's green front door is a partial classic-Mickey shape.

Hint 74: The welcome mat at Mickey's front door is shaped like a classic Mickey.

Hint 75: As you enter the first room, stop by the green, glass-fronted bookcase. The top of the spine of the book "2001: A Mouse Odyssey" is decorated with two gold classic Mickeys.

Hint 76: In the same bookcase, find the orange book, "See You Next Squeak." At the bottom of the spine, the publisher's logo is a classic Mickey enclosed in a square.

Hint 77: At the left side of the first room, the bottom of the spine of the blue book entitled "My Fair Mouse" sports a side-profile Mickey.

Hint 78: Just as you enter the piano room, study the bookcase on the right side. On the right upper shelf, the book "My Life with Walt" has a pink classic Mickey at the top of the spine.

Hint 79: In the same bookcase, locate the book "Pluto's Republic." To its immediate left, a thin green book has a yellow classic Mickey at the top of its spine.

Hint 80: <u>Most of the holes in the paper for the player piano are classic Mickeys, but one of the holes is shaped like Goofy, and another hole is Donald Duck! You can spot Goofy at times through the left side glass, next to the center green</u>

wood post. Donald is visible at times through the right side glass next to the center post. To find Goofy and Donald, you need to look in toward the middle from the sides (left side for Goofy and right side for Donald).

Hint 81: The weight for the metronome on top of the player piano is a Mickey.

Hint 82: Just past the piano, in a cabinet on the left side of the room, a yellow classic Mickey is at the top of the spine of a red book.

Hint 83: In the room with Mickey's drums, look for a drum with legs on the lower shelf. Knobs along its rim sport Mickey ears.

Hint 84: Also in the room with Mickey's drums, Mickey's gloves are on the hour and minute hands of a cuckoo clock on the wall.

Hint 85: There is a mirror on the right side inside *Mickey's Movie Barn*. Stare at it and wait awhile. Mickey Mouse's head will appear.

Hint 86: On your left as you continue walking, a paintbrush on the top right of Donald Duck's wooden workbench has pink paint splotches that form an upside-down classic Mickey.

Hint 87: Also in *Mickey's Movie Barn* (and before you meet Mickey Mouse in person), a classic Mickey appears around the countdown numbers on the screen before the film starts.

Hint 88: Mickey's red car sits outside his house in his driveway. The car's hubcaps and spare tire sport white classic Mickeys.

- In and outside of Minnie's House

Hint 89: Inside the refrigerator in Minnie's kitchen, a bottle of cheese relish on the second shelf in the door has a red classic Mickey "brand mark" at the top of the label.

Hint 90: To the right of the large blue doors that lead backstage near *Minnie's House*, a small opening leads to a "Cast Members Only" entrance and exit. Walk into this opening and look left to spot a blue rock classic Mickey in the wall.

- Toontown Post Office

Hint 91: At the Post Office, Mickey is on the postage stamp on the letter above the entrance. You'll also find a side profile of Mickey (along with five other characters) inside the Post Office on the wall mounted mailboxes. (Twist the mailbox knobs and listen to their reponses!)

- Toontown Fire Department

Hint 92: When you ring the doorbell at the Fire Department, move back quickly to spot the Dalmatian puppy who looks out of an upper middle window for a few seconds. A sideways classic Mickey made of black spots is on his upper forehead.

- Toontown Insurance Company

Hint 93: The doorknob on the brown front door of the bankrupt insurance company is a replica of the doorknob character from the movie "Alice in Wonderland." (A Hidden Surprise!)

Fantasyland

- Alice in Wonderland

Hint 94: As you go down the rabbit hole, watch in front of you for a small house (the White Rabbit's house). A tiny, almost upside-down classic Mickey sits at the upper left corner of a frame (of a picture or mirror) on a wall that you can see through the front window of the upper level of the house. Look in the center of the open window for the Hidden Mickey.

Hint 95: <u>During the next ride segment, stare to your left to spot two small purple mushrooms - the first one in the background and the second one later on and closer to your vehicle. Each mushroom has three white spots on its cap that form a classic Hidden Mickey, and each mushroom is next to an orange mushroom.</u>

Hint 96: When the cards are "painting the roses red," look under the tree to the left, and in front of a ladder, for a slightly distorted red classic Mickey. It's on a second-level ledge under the right hand with the paintbrush and just to the left of an upright green heart.

- Mr. Toad's Wild Ride

Hint 97: On the large statue of Mr. Toad, to the left of the inside entrance queue, tiny red splotches can be seen in the lower part of both corneas (above the white part of the eyes). Both splotches resemble classic Hidden Mickeys, but the one in Mr. Toad's left eye (as you face the statue, it's the eye on the right) is more convincing.

Hint 98: At the beginning of the ride, on the third set of doors that your car drives through, you'll see the head and ears of a tiny dark side-profile Mickey looking to the right. It's in the right door's lower left panel, in the bottom left-most triangle of stained glass. It's hard to spot!

Hint 99: In Winky's Pub, about halfway through the ride, a classic Mickey appears in the foam of the left mug (as you face the scene) spinning above Winky's hand.

Hint 100: The silhouette of Sherlock Holmes can be found in the second-floor window above the Constabulary door; a green frame is around the door. It's in the city room (the room with the fountain) just after you pass through the pub with the bartender who spins the mugs. Once you leave the pub room, look directly to the left and up a little and you'll see Sherlock. (He's not a Disney character, but he is a cool Hidden Surprise!)

- Snow White's Enchanted Wish

Hint 101: A classic Mickey is formed by bushes in the mural directly in front of your ride vehicle at the loading area. Look at the right end of the row of green bushes just past the rocky hill and to the left of the blue stream. The upright classic Mickey is partially hidden by the bush in front.

Hint 102: Early on in the ride, look for the green turtle climbing the stairs to the left of your ride vehicle. The large circle on the left side of the turtle's shell forms the "head" of a three-circle classic Mickey on the shell.

Hint 103: As you pass through the dwarfs' mine, stay alert for the mine car full of bright jewels on your left. A green Tinker Bell is on the back wall behind the mine car, just to the left of the big red jewel held up by a dwarf.

- *Pinocchio's Daring Journey*

Hint 104: <u>As you approach the ride vehicles in the winding entrance queue, stare at the wall mural across the ride track for a green stagecoach headed toward Pleasure Island. A hot-air balloon carrying people floats above Pleasure Island. A brown classic Mickey is in the relief design above the wooden entrance gates to Pleasure Island.</u>

Hint 105: Further along the entrance queue, scan the scene across the ride track for a small flower pot in front of a blue door. Three flowers at the lower right of the group of flowers come together as a classic Hidden Mickey, sideways to the left.

Hint 106: When your vehicle enters the Pleasure Island room, study the ground in front of the popcorn stand on your right. Some "spilled" popcorn forms a classic Hidden Mickey.

Hint 107: Look back at the left side window in the popcorn stand for an upside-down classic Mickey in the popcorn, about one-third the way up in the window.

Hint 108: Near the end of the ride, in Geppetto's workshop, a fish is near the top of a glass globe which sits on a wooden stand covered with ornate carvings. An upright three-circle Hidden Mickey is carved into the right side of the flat upper portion of the stand.

Hint 109: In the next room, a big case holds a model ship. The middle of the top frame of the case is decorated with a wooden classic Mickey.

- Storybook Land Canal Boats

Hint 110: On the middle of one side of the vertical strut at the rear of the "Daisy" boat, an upside-down classic Mickey is made of round flowers—a yellow "head" and pink "ears."

Hint 111: On the "Wendy" boat, a classic Mickey in relief hides on the upper back of the rear post.

Hint 112: On the boat ride, after passing through Monstro the Whale, watch for Pinocchio's Village on your right. As you float in front of the first house in the village, look past this first house and the next blue-roofed house to the rear row of buildings which are visible only for a few seconds. A tiny classic Hidden Mickey is at the upper left of a yellow shield, which is on the left side of the front wall of a building and under a brown roof.

Hint 113: The pumpkin carriage on the upper road approaching Cinderella's village simulates an upside-down classic Mickey. The pumpkin is the "head" and the side wheels are the "ears."

Afternoon Parade

- Grand Marshal automobile

Hint 114: On this attractive replica of an antique touring car, classic Mickeys adorn the tires, the front bumper, the hood ornament, nuts at the side of the front windshield, the tread on the

67

spare tire on the rear of the car, and the brackets holding the spare tire in place.

Frontierland

-Mark Twain Riverboat/ Sailing Ship Columbia

Hint 115: As you cruise along, watch for the second bridge on the left side of the river, and find the second vertical side post (of the wire mesh fence) from the left end of the bridge span. A small classic Hidden Mickey washer is under the second bolt from the top of this post.

Hint 116: Continue to study the bridge. In the shadows under the right side of the bridge is a large black classic Mickey hole in the rock.

Hint 117: Study the metal grillwork between the smokestacks and high above the *Mark Twain's* prow for sideways classic Mickeys.

Hint 118: To the right of the entrance for the *Mark Twain Riverboat* is a "Shipping Office." A painting advertising river excursions on the *Mark Twain* hangs on an outside wall. In the painting, Mickey Mouse is one of the passengers on the lowest deck.

- Tom Sawyer Island

Hint 119: As you exit the Raft onto the island, turn left and look above the first cavern entrance you encounter. A classic Mickey depression is in the rock over the middle of the entrance opening. (You can also spot this Hidden Mickey from the *Mark Twain Riverboat* or the *Sailing Ship Columbia*.)

Hint 120: Stroll into *Dead Man's Grotto* cave. Near the end of the cavern walk-way inside, a jail cell is secured with two Mickey-shaped locks at the ends of a long chain.

Hint 121: Stroll back to the heaps of coins in the *Pirate 's Lair* play area. At the right rear of the coin heaps, look in front of the hanging blue pirate tarp for a wood plank that holds the treasure in place. Three coins on the ground that peek out from under the right side of the wood plank form an upside-down classic Hidden Mickey.

Fantasyland

- *"it's a small world"*

Hint 122: Three circular control towers topped by umbrellas overlook the entrance queue. The center tower is larger than the other two, so together they form a classic Mickey.

Hint 123: Disney characters appear alongside your tour boat. Look for Alice in Wonderland and White Rabbit, Cinderella (across from Alice), Pinocchio, Donald Duck and the Three Caballeros, Ariel and Flounder, Nemo and Dory, Lilo and Stitch, Jessie and Woody, and others.

Hint 124: Early in your boat ride (after Alice in Wonderland and Cinderella), look above you for a boy standing in a hot air balloon with a toy bear holding on to the ropes to the boy's right. The bear's head and ears cast a classic Hidden Mickey shadow on the balloon.

Hint 125: To your left, across from Lilo and Stitch, watch for koala bears hanging on a tree behind a kangaroo. The

head and ears of several of the bears
simulate Mickey's head.

Hint 126: In the last room of the ride,
shadows from groups of small balloons
that move up and down form classic
Mickeys on the ceiling at times above
your boat.

Mickey's Toontown

- Disneyland® Railroad

Hint 127: Spot the agriculture ("Agrifu-
ture") sign from the train just past "it's
a small world" after leaving Mickey's
Toontown station. Above the peach stem
in the sign, the top three grapes in the
bunch of grapes come together to form a
classic Mickey.

Tomorrowland

- Buzz Lightyear Astro Blasters

Hint 128: Two classic Mickeys appear
in the large "Planets of the Galactic
Alliance" mural on the right-side wall
of the entrance queue. One Mickey,
sideways to the left, is located at about
the "10 o'clock" position in the planet
named K'lifooel'ch; it is made of small
green spheres. The other (upside-down)
classic Mickey is made of white spheres
and hides on the right side of the mural above the words "K'tleendon Kan
Cluster."

Hint 129: Along this right-side wall,
look for two "Ska-densii" planets
with side profile "continent" Mickeys.
One is in the "Planets of the Galactic
Alliance" mural, and the second is on
a mural farther along the wall. (This

second mural also has the green-sphere planet described above with the sideways classic Mickey).

Hint 130: Also check out an oblong satellite (called "Green Planet") in the "Planets of the Galactic Alliance" mural—it has an antenna on top and green swirls on the side. Three swirls in the middle of its side form a classic Hidden Mickey, tilted to the left. This planet appears on the wall several times during the ride.

Hint 131: A classic Mickey is etched on a block in the first show room to the left of the vehicle, just past a large rotating wheel and left of a row of target batteries.

Hint 132: A side-profile Mickey hides on a "Ska-densii" planet's continent in the "Planets of the Galactic Alliance" mural on the right-side wall across from the photo-viewing area. If it looks familiar, it's because you see the same Hidden Mickey (as well as the two below) on an entrance-queue mural.

Hint 133: On this same mural on the right wall along the inside exit, look for K'lifooel'ch, the planet formed of many small green spheres. A classic Mickey, sideways to the left, lies along the outer edge of K'lifooel'ch at about the "10 o'clock" location (other classic Mickey spheres are also part of this planet), and an upside-down classic Mickey is formed by three white spheres at the middle right of the mural, above the words "K'tleendon Kan Cluster."

- *Star Tours-The Adventures Continue*

Hint 134: Circles create a Mickey hat with ears on the upper part of the control panel behind C-3PO's head.

Hint 135: In a wall display along the entrance queue, the silhouette of R2-D2 appears several times in a continuous video loop of moving shadow figures. At one point, R2-D2 sprouts satellite ears that rotate into round "Mickey ears" for a few seconds.

Hint 136: Along the entrance queue, a robot watches a continuous scan of luggage moving along a conveyor belt. You can spot images of a plush Mickey Mouse and a plush Goofy, along with images of Buzz Lightyear, Aladdin's lamp, a Sorcerer Mickey hat, a Mr. Incredible shirt, Madame Leota's crystal ball, and others.

Hint 137: Just after you're seated, C-3PO appears in a screen at the front right of the room. A small, bright white classic Mickey is on his right forearm near his wrist.

Hint 138: Coruscant is one of three different and random end destinations for your *Star Tours* journey. As you dive down to the planet and fly among the buildings, stare at the lower right side of the video screen. Three large, faint blue translucent circles come together as a classic Hidden Mickey!

Hint 139: Four more classic Hidden Mickeys can be spotted in the Coruscant landing sequence. After your *Star Tours* vehicle crash lands on a platform and is lowered below into a hanger, look for four recessed panels in the top half of the back wall of the hanger. A classic Mickey is in the center of each panel. To see them, focus on the background wall instead of the droid in the foreground that's flying around with the two light batons.

- Space Mountain

Hint 140: The speakers on the back of the ride-vehicle seats form classic Mickeys.

- Near Finding Nemo Submarine Voyage & the Monorail exit

Hint 141: From the *Disneyland® Monorail* loading area or exit in Tomorrowland, you can often spot a classic Mickey made of coiled rope lying near the end of the Finding Nemo Submarine Voyage dock.

Hint 142: Near the elevator on the ground level, a classic Mickey impression is in the rock wall about one foot off the floor and between two separated handrails.

- Finding Nemo: Marine Observation Outpost

Hint 143: Look for the lockers on the left front wall inside the *Marine Observation Outpost*. You can spot Sorcerer Mickey inside locker No. 105. He's on the clothing that's under a pair of sunglasses.

-Autopia

Hint 144: A black classic Mickey hides in the upper right corner of the car license plates.

- view of Matterhorn Mountain

Hint 145: A large black classic Mickey hole hides in the side of the Matterhorn Mountain. You can see it from various vantage points in Tomorrowland.

Fantasyland

- Pixie Hollow

Hint 146: Near the end of the *Pixie Hollow* waiting queue is a signpost that reads "Fairies Welcome." A classic Mickey is carved out of bark on the front of the signpost, near the bottom.

Critter Country

- The Many Adventures of Winnie the Pooh

Hint 147: The back and lower legs of the "Heffabee" on top of each ride vehicle form an upside-down classic Mickey.

Hint 148: In the first part of the entrance tunnel, a small classic Hidden Mickey hides on the bark of a round tree trunk that you reach just before you get to the wall covered with colorful leaves. Mickey's to the right of your vehicle, at about eye level.

Hint 149: As you leave the Heffalump and Woozle room, turn around in your vehicle and look up behind you to see Max the buck, Buff the buffalo, and Melvin the moose hanging on the wall above you. (These three animals pay homage to the original attractions in this location-the *Country Bear Jamboree* and then the *Country Bear Playhouse*.)

Hint 150: After the Heffalump and Woozle room, there's a Heffalump collage on your right. Look in the bottom right-hand corner to spot an almost upside-down classic Mickey made of yellow bubbles.

- Pooh Corner store

Hint 151: In the room with candies and treats, find a window where you can watch Cast Members prepare treats. On the wall inside and opposite the window are pictures referencing the *Country Bear Jamboree*, which was replaced by *The Many Adventures of Winnie the Pooh*. One picture shows Winnie the Pooh sitting on Gomer the Bear's piano and in another picture, Pooh extends a hand to Teddi Barra. (Hidden Surprise!)

- Briar Patch store

Hint 152: Three yarn balls (white "head" with a white "ear" and a black "ear") come together as a classic Mickey in the middle of a jar sitting on a high shelf at the right rear of the store.

Adventureland

- Walt Disney's Enchanted Tiki Room

Hint 153: Four shields hang over the *Enchanted Tiki Room* exit. A classic Mickey with two smiley faces for "ears" hides near the bottom of the left shield.

Frontierland

- *Entrance walkway from the central hub*

Hint 154: A cannon sits to the right, just past the Frontierland sign on the entrance walkway from the central hub. In the tongue behind the cannon is a classic Mickey, formed by a hole and two bolts.

- *Frontierland Shootin' Exposition*

Hint 155: In front of the "Nancy's Dan" tombstone, three lobes of a cactus resemble a classic Mickey.

- *Pioneer Mercantile shop*

Hint 156: On the walls inside the gift shop, white river rocks at the lower center of some of the lamp covers (the ones with bears) form classic Mickeys.

- *Rancho del Zocalo Restaurante*

Hint 157: Halfway up a wooden support post near the corner of a wall behind a condiment and napkin cart, you can spot a classic Mickey depression in the wood. You'll see it best by looking back in from the exit with the gate on the restaurant's right side (as you approach the restaurant from the main Frontierland walkway).

Fantasyland

- *Fantasy Faire*

Hint 158: Locate Clopin's Music Box for some interesting images. (As a reminder, Clopin is the leader of the gypsies in the Disney movie *The Hunchback of Notre Dame*.) Look to the far left inside the Music Box to spot a tiny classic Mickey at the top of the second window from the left.

Hint 159: Many Disney characters are mixed in the crowd of people inside Clopin's Music Box, including Flynn Rider, Snow White, Doc, Sleepy, Peter Pan, Mr. Smee, Maurice, Belle, the Beast in human form, Gaston, a man from Gaston's tavern, Tony (from Lady and the Tramp), Geppetto, and the evil coachman who takes Pinocchio to Pleasure Island.

- King Arthur Carrousel

Hint 160: Find the white horse, Jingles (with strands of gold jingle bells hanging on its sides). Classic Mickeys made of gemstones are on the front and back of the horse. These classic Mickeys aren't perfectly proportioned, and the "ears" and "head" don't touch, but they seem purposeful. (Jingles is also adorned with images from the *Mary Poppins* movie.)

- The Mad Hatter

Hint 161: Every few minutes, a faint image of the Cheshire Cat appears in the mirror above the store's check-out area.

Hint 162: A Mickey hat with ears hides at one corner of each of two outdoor signs for the shop.

Tomorrowland

- Astro Orbitor

Hint 163: The moving spheres above the *Astro Orbitor* occasionally form classic Mickeys.

- *The Star Trader*

Hint 164: Classic Mickey holes are in some of the shop's upright merchandise display poles.

Hint 165: Some merchandise bins have classic Mickey feet and classic Mickey holes encircling the top rim.

- *Little Green Men Store Command*

Hint 166: A green side profile of Mickey Mouse hides on a planet at the middle right edge of the sign for this store near *Buzz Lightyear Astro Blasters*.

Main Street, U.S.A.

- *Plaza Inn restaurant*

Hint 167: To the right of the main entrance (as you enter), a framed painting of a floral arrangement includes an upside-down classic Mickey formed of roses.

- *Silhouette Studio*

Hint 168: In the front display window of the *Silhouette Studio*, the fancy frames on some of the displays include classic Mickeys. (These frames come and go, but a frame with classic Mickeys is almost always on display.)

- *Fruit cart*

Hint 169: A classic Mickey hides on an axle under a fruit cart that is usually positioned midway along Main Street near the Market House.

- In and near Main Street Cinema

Hint 170: Inside *Main Street Cinema*, some of the recessed lights on the front of the step risers are shaped like classic Mickeys.

Hint 171: Outside, near *Main Street Cinema*, a "Casting Agency" sign on a door includes two classic Mickeys in the design, one at the top and one at the bottom.

- Main Street Magic Shop

Hint 172: Along the front counter inside the *Magic Shop*, a white rope on a display shelf is coiled into a classic Mickey shape.

Hint 173: <u>Cards are stuck on the ceiling. In the middle of the group of cards is an Ace of Clubs, which has a classic Mickey instead of a club at the center of the card.</u>

Hint 174: In an outside display window to the left of the *Magic Shop's* entrance, check out the Ace of Clubs card. A classid Mickey, not a club, is at the center of the card.

- Jolly Holiday Bakery Cafe

Hint 175: <u>Step inside the Cafe, walk toward one of the exit doors, and stand under a light fixture with three lights. Look up to see a classic Mickey configuration of the light covers.</u>

- Penny Arcade

Hint 176: Along the rear wall, a small classic Mickey hides between the play buttons on a game machine called "Pinocchio, Make Him Dance."

- Gibson Girl Ice Cream Parlor

Hint 177: The words "Ice Cream Floats" are on an outside window to the right. A tiny classic Mickey is midway up the right leg of the letter "A" in the word "Floats."

- Emporium store

Hint 178: Walk into the store through the entrance facing Town Square. (It's at the end of the store closest to City Hall.) Look behind the cashier's counter to your right as you enter the store and search the wall for a still-life painting with flowers. A distorted but recognizable image of Sorcerer Mickey is on a blue globe, which sits on a small table in the painting.

Hint 179: Check out a room with toys at the end of the store closest to Carnation Cafe. A toy train makes a circuit on a track above you along the walls. Stand near the small water tower at one corner of the room. Every third or so trip around the track, the train stops in front of the water tower, and a classic Hidden Mickey lights up at the upper right side of the tower. You can also usually spot the faint Hidden Mickey image when it's not lit up.

- above The Mad Hatter

Hint 180: To the left of the Opera House, Disney sculptor Blaine Gibson is honored in one of the middle second-floor windows above *The Mad Hatter*. At the upper part of the window, under the words "The Busy Hands," two hands hold a blue carving. A classic Hidden Mickey forms the right end of the carving.

- *Disneyland® Railroad: Main Street Station*

Hint 181: Classic Mickey-shaped holes are drilled into metal brackets behind the conductor's cabin on top of several of the tender tanks, for example, "Fred Gurley's" Engine No. 3 and "Ward Kimball's" Engine No. 5. You can spot these classic Mickeys from the side waiting queue or from inside the first car.

Frontierland

- *Fantasmic!*

Hint 182: During the *Fantasmic!* show, a classic Mickey appears on the water screen, outlined by white foam. You can spot it at the lower part of the water screen, after Monstro the Whale appears and just before the scene with Mickey and the whirlpool.

Hint 183: A magic mirror is projected on the water screen at one point in the show, and you'll see the faces of various villains in the mirror. Three circles at the bottom of the gold mirror frame come together as a classic Mickey.

Fireworks show

Hint 184: Disneyland's fireworks show often features a cluster of three exploding shells that form a classic Mickey.

Entrance Plaza between the theme parks

Hint 185: Some of the engraved personalized brick plaques at your feet along the entrance plaza feature a bell design. The bell ringer is a classic

Mickey. (You'll also find decorative Mickey images on these plaques.)

Hint 186: Take a look at the directional signpoles. You'll find classic Mickey indentations on the bottoms of some of them, while the tops of the poles sport Mickey ears.

------ **Chapter 3** ------

Disney California Adventure Scavenger Hunt

*
  Arrive at the entrance turnstiles (with your admission ticket) 45 minutes before the opening time for early entry (if you're eligible) or 45 minutes before the official opening time if you're not or if it's a nonearly entry day.

*
  If you want to spend the extra cash, pay for the current version of *Disney Genie+* and/or *Individual Lightning Lane* (you'll pay a separate cost for each one) to enter your chosen attraction's Lightning Lane and accelerate your hunts in the parks. You can access these extra services on the *Disneyland* app (it's free to download) on your smart phone. On certain attractions, however, Hidden Mickeys can only be seen from the Standby (regular) queue. You'll miss them if you take the Lightning Lane route. Therefore, to speed up your hunts even more (if you choose to spend the money), I recommend reserving Lightning Lane (by purchasing the current version of *Disney Genie+*) for one or more of the following:

- *Soarin'* and/or *Incredicoaster*.

Fit your Lightning Lane choice(s) anywhere in my Scavenger Hunt plan. If you

83

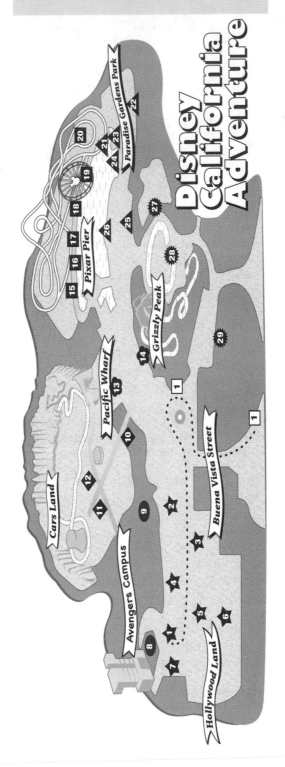

Disney California Adventure®

☐ **Buena Vista Street**
1. Red Car Trolley

⭐ **Hollywood Land**
2. Disney Junior Dance Party
3. Mickey's PhilharMagic
4. Disney Animation:
   Sorcerer's Workshop
   Animation Academy
   Turtle Talk with Crush
5. The Hollywood Backlot Stage
6. Monsters, Inc. Mike & Sulley to the Rescue!
7. Hyperion Theater

⬭ **Avengers Campus**
8. Guardians of the Galaxy – Mission: BREAKOUT!
9. WEB SLINGERS: A Spider-Man Adventure

◆ **Cars Land**
10. Mater's Junkyard Jamboree
11. Luigi's Rollickin' Roadsters
12. Radiator Springs Racers

❁ **Pacific Wharf**
13. The Bakery Tour
14. Walt Disney's Imagineering Blue Sky Cellar

◼ **Pixar Pier**
15. Incredicoaster
16. Jessie's Critter Carousel
17. Toy Story Midway Mania!
18. Games of Pixar Pier
19. Pixar Pal-A-Round
20. Inside Out Emotional Whirlwind

◀ **Paradise Gardens Park**
21. Silly Symphony Swings
22. Goofy's Sky School
23. Jumpin' Jellyfish
24. Golden Zephyr
25. The Little Mermaid –
    Ariel's Undersea Adventure
26. World of Color - ONE

✸ **Grizzly Peak**
27. Redwood Creek Challenge Trail
28. Grizzly River Run
29. Soarin'

85

don't opt for the Lightning Lane options, just follow my Scavenger Hunt plan for efficient touring.

* Hotfoot it to Cars Land. Line up for *Radiator Springs Racers*.

Clue 1: Take note of some cactuses along the standby entrance queue.
3 points

Clue 2: Look for a Hidden Mickey inside the Stanley's Cap 'n' Tap area of the standby entrance queue.
3 points

Clue 3: On the ride, if you go through Ramone's Body Art shop, keep your eyes peeled for Mickey on a wall -mounted electrical box.
5 points

Clue 4: On the ride, if you go through Luigi's tire shop, watch behind Luigi for Hidden Mickeys.
5 points

Clue 5: If you go through Luigi's tire shop, spot Mickey on a red tool box.
5 points

* Ride *Guardians of the Galaxy - Mission: BREAKOUT!*

Clue 6: <u>Search the colorful paint trails on the ground outside the attraction (from the exit around to the entrance, and around the entrance area) for classic Hidden Mickeys.</u>
5 points for 5 or more

Clue 7: Look up for a Hidden Figment in the first room of the entrance queue.
5 points

Clue 8: If you proceed to the right, study display items in the second room for a Mickey face.
5 bonus points

Clue 9: If you approach the far right ride lift on the lower level, look around for a Mickey lock.
3 points

Clue 10: <u>On the ride, don't miss a small black classic Hidden Mickey in the generator control room (with all the electrical cords) at the left side of the screen.</u>
5 points

* Stop by the ***Ancient Sanctum*** where Doctor Strange appears at times.

Clue 11: <u>See any Hidden Mickeys?</u>
2 points

* Pass by Lamplight Lounge and walk to ***Incredicoaster*** and ride if you're brave enough!

Clue 12: While you're screaming, stay alert for a classic Mickey below you on the ground.
4 points

* Line up for ***Toy Story Midway Mania!***
Clue 13: Along the entrance queue, search for a tiny Hidden Mickey on a poster.
4 points

Clue 14: Spot a classic Mickey at the loading dock.
2 points

Clue 15: During the first part of the ride, stay alert for the title of a board game from Walt Disney.
5 points

Clue 16: On an interactive screen as you ride, look behind the target balloons in front of the volcano for a classic Mickey.
5 points

Clue 17: On another screen, watch the white plates for a classic Mickey image.
4 points

Clue 18: Find Mickey after you exit your vehicle.
4 points

* Walk past *Pixar Pal-A-Round* to **Goofy's Sky School**.

Clue 19: As you approach *Goofy's Sky School*, admire a sign for a Hidden Mickey.
2 points

Clue 20: In the standby entrance queue, study two bulletin boards for two subtle Hidden Mickeys.
10 points for finding both

Clue 21: As you exit the ride vehicle, locate Mickey on a tool.
3 points

* Enjoy **Soarin' Around the World** (or **Soarin' Over California** - see below).

Clue 22: Pay attention to the pre-show video for Mickey ears.
2 points

Clue 23: Also in the pre-show video, find some clothing characters.
4 points for spotting two Hidden Characters

Clue 24: During the ride, search the hills to the left of the castle in Germany

for a Hidden Mickey near a footbridge.
5 points

Clue 25: Focus on the desert sky for a
floating Hidden Mickey.
5 points

Clue 26: Study the Fiji island for a small
classic Mickey.
5 points

Clue 27: Look for some floating Mickeys
below you near the end of the ride.
4 points

Clue 28: A huge classic Mickey in the sky
greets you at the end of your ride.
3 points

[If *Soarin' Over California* is showing –
Clue 29: Pay attention to the pre-show
video for Mickey ears.
2 points

Clue 30: Also in the pre-show video, find
some clothing characters.
4 points for spotting two Hidden Characters

Clue 31: While on the ride, look left for
a Mickey balloon when you spot the golf
course.
4 points

Clue 32: Now quickly look right for a
Mickey shadow on the golf course.
4 points

Clue 33: Watch the golf ball hurtling
toward you.
5 points

Clue 34: Look for some floating Mickeys below you near the end of the ride.
4 points

Clue 35: A huge classic Mickey in the sky greets you at the end of your ride.
5 points]

* Over in Cars Land, enter the queue for *Mater's Junkyard Jamboree*.

Clue 36: Search above you for a classic Mickey.
4 points

Clue 37: While in the queue, glance around the ride surface area for a Hidden Mickey, then enjoy the attraction if you wish. Or exit without riding to search for the next Hidden Mickey.
3 points

* Check out the entrance queue for *Luigi 's Rollickin' Roadsters*.

Clue 38: Look for a tiny Lightning McQueen with Mickey ears.
4 points

Clue 39: Find a drawing of a small red car with a Mickey-shaped headlight.
4 points

Clue 40: Search nearby for an upside-down classic Mickey.
3 points

* Consider lunch at the restaurant of your choice or try one of the counter-service eateries such as Flo's V8 Cafe, Pacific Wharf Cafe, Cocina Cucamonga Mexican Grill, or Paradise Garden Grill.
- While at lunch, check your Times Guide or Disneyland app for convenient show times for *Disney Junior Dance Party* and the *Five & Dime show* in Carthay Circle.

*
   Stroll to Paradise Gardens Park and enjoy *The Little Mermaid - Ariel's Undersea Adventure*.

Clue 41: Look for Mickey along the outside entrance queue.
2 points

Clue 42: Can you see Mickey in the lights?
2 points

Clue 43: In the entrance queue, search for a classic Mickey on top of a scallop shell.
3 points

Clue 44: Don't miss the Hidden Mickey on the loading dock mural!
4 points

Clue 45: As you enter the room where the "Under the Sea" song is playing, study the purple coral for a classic Mickey.
4 points

Clue 46: Watch the spinning purple octopus for a Hidden Mickey.
4 points

Clue 47: Three Hidden Images are near the singing Ariel. Stare below her for the first one: a coral Hidden Mickey.
4 points

Clue 48: Locate a green fish nearby who is wearing a small, blue classic Mickey.
5 points

Clue 49: Now look quickly to your right across the track for a Hidden Mr. Limpet!
5 points

Clue 50: Check out the frogs along the ride!
4 points for one or more

Clue 51: Now look behind the frogs for a Hidden Mickey in the water.
4 points

Clue 52: Stay alert for a Hidden Surprise (two silhouettes) at the end of the ride, just before you exit your clam-mobile. It's a tribute to The Little Mermaid.
5 points

*
Go to **Monsters, Inc. Mike & Sulley to the Rescue!** and line up.

Clue 53: Study the inside queue walls for a Hidden Mickey.
3 points

Clue 54: Watch the pre-show video monitor in the queue for a Hidden Mickey.
3 points

Clue 55: Before you board your vehicle, spot those headlights again!
2 points

Clue 56: At the beginning of the ride, search the skyline for a tiny Mickey.
5 points

Clue 57: Don't miss the moving Mickey shadow on a wall along the ride! Concentrate on the left wall.
5 points

Clue 58: Admire the color-changing Randall (the multi-legged lizard-shaped monster) for a Hidden Mickey!
5 bonus points

Clue 59: On the ride, look for a Hidden Mickey on Sulley.
4 points

Clue 60: Stay alert for Mickey near a monitor screen.
3 points

* It's time for more Hollywood Land magic! Mosey into **Mickey's PhilharMagic**.

Clue 61: In the show, look for a shadow Mickey on a table.
4 points

Clue 62: Stare at Ariel's jewels for a classic Mickey in a ring.
5 points

Clue 63: Keep alert for a classic Mickey during the magic carpet ride.
5 points

* At a convenient time, visit **Disney Junior Dance Party**.

Clue 64: <u>Look up inside for the largest Hidden Mickey in the Dance Party!</u>
3 points

Clue 65: <u>Watch for small Mickey images on stage and on the main screen during the show.</u>
5 points for spotting five or more

Clue 66: Find some Hidden Mickeys in a window of the *Disney Junior Dance Party* building.
3 points for 2 small Hidden Mickeys

* Amble over to Carthay Circle for the **Five & Dime show** you selected.

Clue 67: If the performers are in a car, study the car for Hidden Mickeys.
3 points

* Enter Hollywood Land, then stand outside the **Disney Animation Building**.

Clue 68: Look up for a Hidden Mickey on a pole.
3 points

Clue 69: Now search for Mickey on the outside wall of the *Animation Building*.
2 points total for one or more

Clue 70: Search for a classic Hidden Mickey high above the stage inside the *Animation Academy*.
3 points

Clue 71: While inside *Animation Academy*, look for another classic Mickey on the Animator's desk.
2 points

Clue 72: Don't leave yet! Notice anything in the carpet?
3 points

*Walk through the *Sorcerer's Workshop*.

Clue 73: <u>Check out Hidden Mickeys on some tables.</u>
2 points

Clue 74: Locate two Hidden Mickeys on the wall.
4 points for spotting both

Clue 75: Stroll back to the *Beast's Library* for a hot Hidden Mickey.
2 points

Clue 76: Spot Hidden Mickeys along the *Animation Building's* exit hall.
3 points total for one or more

Clue 77: Find a Hidden Mickey in a wall poster outside.
2 points

Clue 78: Look for Mickey on the ceiling inside the *Off the Page* store.
4 points

* Cross the street to **Schmoozies**.

Clues 79, 80, and 81: Check out the outside walls for Hidden Mickeys.
5 points total for finding three Hidden Mickeys

Clue 82: Spot Minnie Mouse behind the order windows!
5 points

* Walk over to **The Bakery Tour** in Pacific Wharf.

Clue 83: Look around for Mickey inside the entrance to the Tour.
2 points

* Approach **Walt Disney Imagineering Blue Sky Cellar**.
Wander behind *Blue Sky Cellar*.

Clue 84: Outside *Blue Sky Cellar*, look for Mickey in Pinot Grigio grapes.
4 points

* Mosey to the **Redwood Creek Challenge Trail** in Grizzly Peak.

Clue 85: Tarry at the large trail map just inside the entrance and spot three classic Mickeys.
5 points for finding all three

Clue 86: Find a Mickey reference in the Mt. Whitney Lookout.
5 points

*Walk past the entrance to **Grizzly River Run** to the fence overlooking the raft stream.

Clue 87: Investigate the area near the fence for a Hidden Mickey.
4 points

*Walk to Cars Land.

Clue 88: Gaze inside the office of the **Cozy Cone Motel** for a Hidden Cars movie character and a Hidden Mickey.
5 points for both

Clue 89: Mater poses at times for photos near the motel. Study him for a Hidden Mickey.
3 points

Clue 90: Outside the **Radiator Springs Curios Store**, check around for a classic Hidden Mickey.
5 points

Clue 91: Find a classic Mickey on the wall inside *Radiator Springs Curios Store*.
2 points

Clue 92: Glance up for Mickey inside the store.
2 points

* Spend some time studying the six colorful car hoods in the outside display windows of **Ramone's House of Body Art**. (These car hoods may switch places to different windows at times.)

Clues 93 to 98: Mickey hides somewhere on each car hood! Start with the rightmost display window (as you face the storefront from outside).
30 points for finding all six

Clue 99: Admire the purple car hood behind the front counter inside *Ramone's* and try to find Mickey.
5 points

Clue 100: Now spot Mickey on pillars inside the store.
2 points

Clue 101: Look around for Mickey images on merchandise boxes.
4 points for one or more

Clue 102: Outside *Ramone's House of Body Art*, search for Mickey near a pole.
4 points

*
Head to Pixar Pier and locate the **Poultry Palace.**

Clue 103: <u>Don't miss a Hidden Mickey in the short queue!</u>
3 points

Now watch the action at **Jessie's Critter Carousel**.

Clue 104: Study an armadillo in an inner circle for a Hidden Mickey.
4 point

*
Step over to the **Jack-Jack Cookie Num Num**s stand.

Clue 105: Do you see a Hidden Mickey on a cookie?
3 points

*
Stroll past *Incredicoaster* along the promenade.

Clue 106: Search for an upside-down Hidden Mickey on a billboard.
3 points

97

*   Return to Buena Vista Street to find more Hidden Mickeys.

Clue 107: Look down along the entrance area in front of **Carthay Circle Restaurant** for a Hidden Mickey.
5 points

Clue 108: Inside **Clarabelle's Hand-Scooped Ice Cream Shop**, search for Mickey on a display bottle.
5 points

Clue 109: Find a Hidden Mickey in a window of the **Julius Katz & Sons** store.
2 points

Clue 110: Inside *Julius Katz & Sons*, search a top shelf for a Hidden Mickey.
4 points

Clue 111: Inside **Big Top Toys** store, locate a Hidden Mickey on a mural.
4 points

Clue 112: Near **Oswald's**, scan a blue advertisement on an outside wall for Mickey.
5 points

Clue 113: Spot a classic Mickey at the **Red Car Trolley Station** near the main park entrance.
3 points

*   Exit Disney California Adventure Park to the **main entrance plaza**.

Clue 114: Look over the trees in the entrance plaza for Hidden Mickeys.
3 points

Clue 115: Check out some ticket buildings for Hidden Mickeys.
2 points

*Enjoy dinner at the restaurant of your choice.

Now total your score.

Total Points for Disney California Adventure Park =

How'd You Do?

Up to 170 points - Bronze
171 to 340 points - Silver
341 points and over - Gold
425 points - Perfect Score

You may have done even better if you earned bonus points in *Monsters, Inc. Mike & Sulley to the Rescue!* or in *Guardians of the Galaxy – Mission: BREAKOUT!*

If you need help, the Hints are here for you!

Cars Land
- *Radiator Springs Racers*

Hint 1: A classic Mickey made of three barrel cactuses sits on the ground along the right side of the standby entrance queue. It's just past a pole with a sign that says "Long Trip? One Sip and Watch Those Miles Melt Away."

Hint 2: Inside the Stanley's Cap 'n' Tap covered area along the standby entrance queue, a wedding photo of Stanley and Lizzie is on a wall. A classic Mickey is formed of circles above Lizzie's forehead in the middle of her veil.

Hint 3: On the ride, if you go through Ramone's Body Art shop, look back to your right in the second room of the shop to spot a classic Mickey made of circles on an electrical box. It's on the right rear wall just past the doors between the rooms of Ramone's shop.

Hint 4: On the ride, if you go through Luigi's tire shop, glance in the window behind Luigi to spot moving light images that include small classic Mickey shapes.

Hint 5: Also in Luigi's tire shop, watch on your right for a red toolbox that sits behind a rack of tires. Three inner circles in a design on the side of the box form a classic Mickey.

Avengers Campus

- *Guardians of the Galaxy- Mission: BREAKOUT!*

Hint 6: <u>Outside the attraction, colorful trails on the ground were formed when Rocket Raccoon spilled paint during an escape. Classic Hidden Mickeys are scattered in the colorful paint splotches along these trails.</u>

Hint 7: Inside the first room along the entrance queue, various creatures are imprisoned in electrified glass cases suspended from the ceiling. You can barely make out Figment's head and arms as he stands in a case (usually with light brown lighting) in the middle of the left side (as you face the video screen across the room) of the group of cases above you.

Hint 8: On the right side, in the second room (the Collector's office), along the wall to your left as you enter, look for a caged display cabinet. A small black-and-white Mickey face (possibly on a ceramic mug) stares back at you from behind a green vase sitting at the left side of the third shelf.

Hint 9: A Mickey-shaped lock is attached to a horizontal valve wheel near the rightmost ride lift on the lower level.

Hint 10: On the ride, at one point you pause in front of a generator control room with electrical cords hanging and strewn all over the room. At the far upper left of the screen, a black classic Hidden Mickey is on a small rectangular box, to the right of an orange circle and above a green waveform.

- Doctor Strange and the Ancient Sanctum

Hint 11: Inside the Ancient Sanctum where Doctor Strange appears, large circles on the ground of the courtyard come together as classic Mickeys.

Pixar Pier

- Incredicoaster

Hint 12: When you're upside down in the loop, look at the ground to your left for a classic Mickey cement footing at the base of one of the vertical support poles. You can also spot this Mickey if you look right as you ride through the little hills that cover the *Toy Story Midway Mania!* attraction building.

- Toy Story Midway Mania!

Hint 13: Along the inside part of the winding entrance queue, spots near a blue dinosaur's left eye and upper horn form a classic Mickey, tilted to the right.

The dino, Trixie from *Toy Story*, is near the right lower corner of a poster labeled "Dino Darts."

Hint 14: On the wall at the loading area, a classic Mickey is formed by three picture frames with *Toy Story* characters.

Hint 15: At the beginning of the ride, right after the practice round and as your vehicle scoots to the next stop, look back at the wall behind you for a Hidden Surprise: "Walt Disney's Adventureland game," which sits flat below the "Twister" game.

Hint 16: Watch for the screen with target balloons in front of the volcano spewing lava. If you pop the middle 100-point balloon on the second tier, a faint classic Mickey appears on the rear surface in the lava behind the balloons.

Hint 17: Be alert for the screen with moving white plates. At one point, a large front plate aligns with smaller plates behind it to form a classic Mickey.

Hint 18: Along the exit walkway from the ride, a "Toy Story Midway" game sits on a rug in a display room to the left. On the left side of the game box, three ovals (containing pictures of Jessie, Rex, and Bullseye the horse) form a classic Mickey.

Paradise Gardens Park

- *Goofy's Sky School*

Hint 19: As you walk toward *Goofy's Sky School*, look up at a sign for the attraction that shows Goofy flying a red plane. Three large holes in the sign form a sideways classic Mickey.

Hint 20: Along the standby entrance queue, check the walls for cork bulletin boards. On the first board, three round impressions in the cork form a classic Mickey. It's tilted to the right, and it's at the right lower side of the upside-down note that says, "Notice to Appear." A similar classic Hidden Mickey made of impressions is on a second bulletin board on another wall along the queue. This one is tilted to the left and is partially covered by the left side of a handwritten letter that says "Dear Teach." Look above the right upper corner of a note that reads "I Fix Planes!" to spot it.

Hint 21: As you exit the ride vehicle, look for a classic Mickey at the top of the handle of a wrench that's hanging on a wall at the far right of a tool rack.

Grizzly Peak

- *Soarin' Around the World*

Hint 22: In the pre-show video, a man is asked to remove his Mickey Mouse ears.

Hint 23: Also in the pre-show, a boy sitting in his ride seat is wearing a shirt with a Grumpy logo and shorts sporting Mickey Mouse.

Hint 24: Early in the film, you'll approach a castle in Germany. Look to the left in the distance at a footbridge that crosses a chasm. To the right of the far end of the footbridge, a black classic Mickey marking is on the edge of the hill at about the same level as the bridge.

Hint 25: In the scene with hot air balloons floating above the desert, three colorful balloons in the distance merge together as a classic Hidden Mickey. The image is visible for only a few seconds.

Hint 26: When you approach the round Fiji island, focus on the beach right in front of you. Three small rocks near the lower right edge of the beach come together as a classic Mickey, tilted slightly to the left.

Hint 27: As you fly over Disneyland's Main Street, U. S.A. near the end of the ride, some people walking below you are carrying Mickey balloons.

Hint 28: As you approach Sleeping Beauty Castle, watch for a classic Mickey made of bursts of white fireworks over the Castle.

- [*Soarin' Over California*

Hint 29: In the pre-show video, a man is asked to remove his Mickey Mouse ears.

Hint 30: Also in the pre-show, a boy sitting in his ride seat is wearing a shirt with a Grumpy logo and shorts sporting Mickey Mouse.

Hint 31: When you soar over the hills and spot a golf course, look immediately to your lower left and find a golf cart. The man standing on the other side of the cart is holding a blue Mickey balloon.

Hint 32: Now look fast to the right side of the golf course. About halfway along the fairway, a slightly distorted classic Mickey shadow is cast on the green grass by a cluster of three trees. The "ears" of the shadow Mickey touch the right side of the white cart path.

Hint 33: Stare straight ahead and down to the golf course. Spot the man about to swing a golf club. When he strikes the golf ball, it will head directly toward you. Don't blink! Watch the ball's rotation to see the dark classic Mickey on the surface of the ball.

Hint 34: As you fly over Disneyland's Main Street, U. S.A. near the end of the ride, some people walking below you are carrying Mickey balloons.

Hint 35: As you approach Sleeping Beauty Castle, watch for a classic Mickey made of bursts of white fireworks over the Castle.]

Cars Land

- *Mater's Junkyard Jamboree*

Hint 36: Three hubcaps form a classic Mickey, tilted to the left, in the entrance queue of *Mater 's Junkyard Jamboree*. As you enter the covered area of the queue, they're above you at the far left corner near the ceiling.

Hint 37: Further along the queue, you can see three barrels inside the ride area that are positioned and proportioned to form a classic Mickey standing upright. A red barrel serves as the "head."

- *Luigi's Rollickin' Roadsters*

Hint 38: Along the entrance queue, as you enter the second room inside, look for collages on the right wall. Behind glass, in the third collage from the right, a tiny red Lightning McQueen antenna topper has a Mickey hat with ears on its roof. This antenna topper is in the right middle part of the collage, below a white

107

piece of paper on which someone has written "# 121."

Hint 39: In the same room, the fourth glass covered collage from the right has a red car with a sideways classic Mickey headlight. The car is above a sign for Buckingham Palace, in the right middle of the collage.

Hint 40: Also in this fourth collage, near the left upper corner, a green and blue round symbol above two silver gears with red decals looks to be an upside-down classic Mickey. Find it above the word "Paris."

Paradise Gardens Park

- *The Little Mermaid - Ariel's Undersea Adventure*
Hint 41: Classic Mickey circles hide in the design of the ironwork along the sides of the upper support for the entrance queue cover.

Hint 42: As you enter the queue inside the building, the globes in the chandeliers merge together from certain vantage points to form classic Mickeys.

Hint 43: As you approach the loading dock area along the entrance queue, you pass under an arch with an orange scallop shell painted on it. Two gold scepters project from the top of the shell. Three light green circles just above the top middle of the shell come together as an upside-down classic Mickey.

Hint 44: A small classic Mickey is impressed in a large rock at the lower left corner of the loading dock mural, just above the green tile. You can spot this Hidden Mickey from the entrance queue and again as you pass by it on your right in your seashell vehicle.

Hint 45: Just before you enter the room where the song "Under the Sea" is playing, a collection of purple coral appears to your left above some star-fish on a brown rock outcropping. A classic Mickey is formed by three holes on the upper part of the top round coral.

Hint 46: In the same room, three pink spots near the middle of the spinning purple octopus's head form a sideways classic Mickey, tilted to the right.

Hint 47: As you move around the sing-ing Ariel, stare at the standing tubular coral stalks below her. In the middle of the group of corals, the round tops of three stalks form a classic Mickey tilted to the right.

Hint 48: Just past Ariel, watch for a green fish with a tall purple turban hat who is dancing with Flounder (the yellow and blue fish). This green fish has a large, oval yellow earring on her left ear, and at the top of the earring is a small, blue classic Mickey.

Hint 49: As soon as you pass Flounder, look quickly over your right shoulder - across the track from Flounder - for a blue Hidden Mr. Limpet (Don Knotts as a fish from "The Incredible Mr. Limpet" movie). He's wearing glasses and peeking out from the green sea-weed. (Not a Hidden Mickey, but a cool Hidden Surprise!)

Hint 50: Toward the end of the ride, check the pond (to your right) for frogs with dark spots on their backs that form sideways classic Mickeys.

Hint 51: To the rear left of the boat with Ariel and Eric and behind the frogs and fish, three lily pads form a classic Mickey on the water.

Hint 52: Another Hidden Surprise – a Hidden Tribute - awaits you at the end of the ride, right before you exit your clam-mobile. In a small recess in the wall to your left, silhouettes on dark brown cabinet doors outline Hans Christian Andersen (on the door to the left) and The Little Mermaid statue in Copenhagen, Denmark (on the door to the right). "The Little Mermaid" was one of the fairy tales written by Danish author Hans Christian Andersen.

Hollywood Land

- Monsters, Inc. Mike & Sulley to the Rescue!

Hint 53: On the "Monstropolis Cab Co." wall poster, the taxicab headlights form an upside-down classic Mickey.

Hint 54: During the video loop on the queue monitors, a taxi appears with the words "Please Proceed" on the front bumper. The headlights of this vehicle are shaped like upside-down classic Mickeys.

Hint 55: The taxi with the upside-down headlight classic Mickeys is pictured on the side of your vehicle.

Hint 56: As your vehicle begins to move, look at the skyline behind a tall wall to your left. A tiny black classic Mickey is visible through holes along the top of the wall. Look along the skyline. You'll find this Mickey below the green "Downtown" sign and to the left of a tall vertical pipe behind the wall.

Hint 57: To the left of your ride vehicle, a side-profile shadow of the main mouse moves from left to right—also a smaller side profile shadow of Mickey moves from right to left—along the windows in the wall of the Harryhausen's restaurant scene. (Try to spot his moving shadow on the right wall, too!)

Hint 58: Watch for "Boo" on top of Randall's back. She pounds on Randall's head with a bat, causing his camouflage coloration to change continually. At one point, his body turns lime green (or sometimes yellow) with a blue (or purple) classic Mickey spot on his belly above a lower leg. (Note: This great image is visible only intermittently and not on every ride-through. Good luck!)

Hint 59: Sulley appears several times during the ride. A dark classic Mickey marking is on Sulley's left leg the last time he appears (by the pink door with the blue flower on it).

Hint 60: Near the end of the ride, a classic Mickey is formed by dials and gauges on a control panel under the right monitor screen.

- Mickey's PhilharMagic

Hint 61: In the "Be Our Guest" portion of the movie, there is a point where you are watching Lumiere dancing on the table with other characters. The view goes to an overhead shot and there are shadows cast on the table from the candle hands of Lumiere. These shadows come together at times to form what appear to be Hidden Mickeys.

Hint 62: In "The Little Mermaid" segment, Ariel throws jewels out into the water in front of her. Focus on the gold ring to the right (your right) of Ariel. A dark classic Mickey is visible just as you first spot the open center of the ring as it starts rotating. The center hole in the ring becomes round—not Mickey-shaped—as the ring completes its rotation.

Hint 63: Watch closely as Aladdin and Jasmine ride their magic carpet in the sky. Stare at the bottom left of the screen for a quick glimpse of three buildings on the ground. Their bright domes are clustered together as a classic Mickey. The lower dome sits in a larger round dark circle to form the "head" of the Hidden Mickey.

- Disney Junior Dance Party

Hint 64: <u>Circular light fixtures hanging from the ceiling come together for the largest Hidden Mickey inside. The central circle forms a classic Mickey with the smaller circles.</u>

Hint 65: <u>Small classic Mickeys (usually) decorate the costumes of the dance instructors and appear on the main screen during the live show, like on Mickey's racecar and in bubbles, etc. (Many decor Mickeys are scattered around inside the dance room.)</u>

Hint 66: In the front leftmost outside window of the *Disney Junior Dance Party* building, facing the street, is a display for "Mickey and the Roadster Racers" (a Disney children's TV show). A small classic Mickey is on Mickey's uniform and classic Mickeys are on the front of his racecar. Several larger decorative (not hidden) classic Mickey images are in the display.

Buena Vista Street

- *Five & Dime show*

Hint 67: The *Five & Dime show* musicians are often performing in a vehicle, and this vehicle's tires have classic Mickeys in the tread.

Hollywood Land

- *Disney Animation Building*

Hint 68: A small classic Mickey sits atop the flagpole over the front of the *Animation Building*.

Hint 69: Along the top of some outside windows and wall pillars, classic Mickey "hats" are in the tile design.

Hint 70: A drum set shaped like a classic Mickey sits on a shelf high above the stage inside the *Animation Academy*.

Hint 71: A red classic Mickey-shaped picture frame is on the top shelf at the middle of the Animator's desk on the left side of the stage. (You'll also find many decorative Mickey images on and around the stage.)

Hint 72: Side-profile Mickeys (a bit abstract) are repeated in the pattern of the stage carpet. (Be aware that carpets are changed from time to time).

Hint 73: In the *Sorcerer's Workshop*, classic Mickeys are along the sides of several long, rectangular containers on tables.

Hint 74: Also in the *Sorcerer's Workshop*, Sorcerer Mickey is on the left wall toward the end of the room. He's encircled by classic Mickey bubbles. Nearby on the left wall, you'll find a classic Mickey intertwined with the middle of a treble clef.

Hint 75: In the *Beast's Library*, just past the Sorcerer's Workshop, a classic Mickey design is in the upper middle of the grate in front of a faux fireplace.

Hint 76: In the mosaic lettering on the exit walls, large and small circles form many classic Mickeys.

Hint 77: The shadow of a person with Mickey ears appears at the bottom of the "Character Close-up" poster on the wall outside.

- Off the Page shop

Hint 78: On a drawing hanging from the ceiling in the middle of *Off the Page*, bubbles form a classic Mickey in front of the shadow of an alligator's front leg.

- Schmoozies
Hint 79: Face *Schmoozies* from the street, and then walk to the left side of the store. There are two murals on the left wall. The one on the right has classic Mickeys formed by small round green and white pieces of colored glass.

Hint 80: Now face the shop from Hollywood Boulevard. A classic Mickey formed by three tan stones hides to the right of a knife tip and above a pink cup on the right side of the rightmost mural on the front of the shop.

Hint 81: Near the center of the mosaic mural closest to Fairfax Market, a red jewel with two button ears forms a classic Mickey. It's to the right of the word "EAT."

Hint 82: On the rear wall directly behind the front smoothie order windows, a Hidden Minnie Mouse decked out as the Statue of Liberty is in the middle and near the top of the wall mosaic.

Pacific Wharf

- The Bakery Tour

Hint 83: On a table in a corner of the first room, you'll see bread rolls. Sometimes they're shaped like Mickey; other times they're imprinted with him.

-Walt Disney Imagineering Blue Sky Cellar

Hint 84: Along an outside walkway behind *Blue Sky Cellar*, three grapes in a painting of white wine grapes form a classic Mickey on the left branch at the upper left of a group of Pinot Grigio grapes.

Grizzly Peak

- Redwood Creek Challenge Trail

Hint 85: You'll find three classic Mickeys on the left side of the trail map. A group of three rocks in a stream forms a Hidden Mickey at the top left of the map. Three circles in the middle left form a classic Mickey in foam (look just to the left of the mouth of the left water slide). Lower down, three log seats in the Ahwahnee Camp Circle are arranged to create a classic Mickey.

Hint 86: Climb the stairs to the Mt. Whitney Lookout and check out the phonetic spelling alphabet (also known as the NATO phonetic alphabet and more accurately as the International Radiotelephony Spelling Alphabet) on a sheet of paper atop a table in the Lookout room. The word for "M" in the official phonetic spelling alphabet is "Mike." But this is Disney! So, the word for "M" is, you guessed it – "Mickey"!

- Near Grizzly River Run entrance

Hint 87: A classic Mickey made of rocks is embedded in the pavement under the right side of the fence, close to the "Grizzly Peak Recreation Area" cabin.

Cars Land

- Cozy Cone Motel

Hint 88: Inside the *Cozy Cone Motel* office, Buzz Lightyear peeks out from under an orange cone on a shelf at the end of a counter. He can be spotted from a rear window of the office, which is locked and closed to guests. A Hidden Mickey figurine is on the lower shelf at the other end (the front) of the counter. (Note: At times, you may spot other Hidden Characters on these shelves.)

- Residents of Radiator Springs Greeting Area

Hint 89: The wing nut on Mater's engine air filter has Mickey ears.

- Radiator Springs Curios Store

Hint 90: On the far left lower wall of the front porch of *Radiator Springs Curios Store*, a classic Mickey is on the upper right outer edge of a yellow "Pump" sign. (Note: Sometimes this sign is partially hidden by furniture or other objects on the porch.)

Hint 91: Inside the store, on the wall to the right of the cashier, a yellow "Service" sign and two round red hubcaps form a classic Mickey.

Hint 92: Some groups of circles on the ceiling inside the store form classic Mickeys.

- Ramone's House of Body Art store

Hint 93: In the outside display window at the far right of the storefront, a white classic Mickey is in the lacy fabric at the lower middle of a car hood.

Hint 94: In the next window, the second window from the far right, spot a car hood with orange and yellow "flames." A faint classic Mickey hides on the far right side of the hood under the rightmost blue vertical streak.

Hint 95: In the third window from the far right, a tiny white classic Hidden Mickey is at the middle bottom of a brown car hood with a pinstripe design. You have to look very low to see this one!

Hint 96: Moving to your left to the third window from the far left, another car hood hosts a faint white classic Mickey. It's on the right side, in the bottom red fringe of the second blue-and-red vertical design from the right.

Hint 97: In the second outside display window from the far left, a subtle white classic Mickey hides in the red flame in the lower middle of a bronze and white car hood. It's in a trough of the flame just to the right of midline. This Hidden Mickey is very hard to spot!

117

Hint 98: In the leftmost outside display window of *Ramone's House of Body Art*, a small white classic Mickey, tilted to the right, lies in a light yellow square area about halfway up the right side of the car hood.

Hint 99: Inside the store, a faint white classic Mickey is on the right side of a purple car hood that stands behind the front sales counter. It's just above and to the far right of the word "Ramone's."

Hint 100: Classic Mickeys are part of the decorative pinstripe design on the support pillars inside Ramone's.

Hint 101: Subtle classic Mickeys are traced on a few paint-splattered boxes on the floor and on shelves inside the store.

- Near the Fire Department building

Hint 102: A sideways classic Mickey is high up on a power line that hangs on a telephone pole to the left of the statue of Stanley the car, near the *Town of Radiator Springs Fire Department building*.

Pixar Pier

- Poultry Palace

Hint 103: <u>On the top of the silver metal queue pole closest to the order window of the *Poultry Palace*, three dark circular marks are positioned to form a classic Mickey.</u>

- Jessie's Critter Carousel

Hint 104: On the blue armadillo in the second circle (inside the outer circle), a classic Mickey made of spots sits on the right front shoulder area.

- Jack-Jack Cookie Num Nums

Hint 105: At the rear of the cookie stand is a mural that shows Jack-Jack holding a cookie that has three chocolate chips shaped as a classic Mickey.

- Along the promenade

Hint 106: One of the billboards along the promenade between Incredicoaster and the Adorable Snowman Frosted Treats shop is titled "Keep Our Pier Beautiful." On the left side of the poster, baby otters are holding a plastic six-pack can holder. The reflection of the six-pack holder in the water reveals an upside-down classic Mickey.

Buena Vista Street

- 1901 Lounge

Hint 107: A tiny white classic Hidden Mickey hides in the white tile in front of the entrance door to the *1901 Lounge* next to the entrance to *Carthay Circle Restaurant*.

- Clarabelle's Hand-Scooped Ice Cream Shop

Hint 108: Along a rear wall inside the shop, the cows on the Clarabelle's Dairy Milk bottles displayed behind the counter have classic Mickey spots on their sides.

- Julius Katz & Sons store

Hint 109: In an outside display window of the store, a classic Mickey image is on a test pattern on a television screen.

Hint 110: Inside the store, a classic Mickey image is formed by the ends of rollers on a small silver mechanical device, which sits on a top shelf along a wall to the right as you enter from Buena Vista Street.

- Big Top Toys store

Hint 111: Inside the store, a gray classic Hidden Mickey, tilted to the right, hides on the dapple horse at the lower middle of the mural behind the cashier's counter. The Hidden Mickey is located on the right side of the horse's neck, just above the decorative orange reins.

- near Oswald's

Hint 112: On a wall above and to the right of the Chamber of Commerce building near *Oswald's*, a blue painted advertisement says "Elias and Company, Open 7 Days." A tiny white classic Mickey hides along the inner border of the blue area, to the right of the "N" in "Open."

- Buena Vista Street Trolley Station

Hint 113: At the trolley station waiting area near the main park entrance, a classic Mickey made of rocks hides in the support pillar nearest the park entrance. It's under the four vertical red bricks, which are at the top of the outer right side of the pillar nearest the street. This Hidden Mickey is tilted to the left, and the left "ear" has striped markings.

Main Entrance Plaza

Hint 114: Ironwork gratings surround some tree trunks in the entrance plaza. Tiny classic Mickey fasteners hold a few of the ironwork bands in place.

Hint 115: You'll find classic Mickey holes inside the braces that support the plaza's ticket-booth counters.

Chapter 4

Downtown Disney District & Resort Hotel Scavenger Hunt

Because you may want to hunt only one area at a time, I've listed the perfect score for each area in parentheses after its name in the Clues section.

Remember to check out any hotel or shop carpets or rugs (which are changed periodically) for Hidden Mickeys.

Downtown Disney District
(11 points)

*   Begin your Downtown Disney search at the entrance across from the *Disneyland Hotel* at about 11:00 a.m.

*   Enter **Splitsville Luxury Lanes**.

Clue 1: Locate a Hidden Mickey near the bowling lanes on the lower level.
3 points

Clue 2: Now search the upper level walls for a classic Hidden Mickey.
3 points

*   Your next stop is **Marceline's Confectionery**.

Clue 3: Find a Hidden Mickey outside the store.
3 points

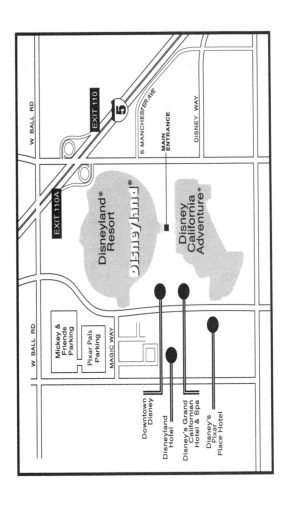

Clue 4: Study the **kiosks** near the entrance plaza.
2 points

*
Now head for the **Mickey & Friends Parking Structure** area to find more Hidden Mickeys. You can walk there or take a tram from Downtown Disney.

Mickey & Friends Parking Structure
(6 points)

Clue 5: Stop and look up at the directional sign on the walkway near the tram stop.
2 points

Clue 6: <u>Spot classic Mickeys inside the parking garage next to the security checkpoint area.</u>
2 points

Hop on the tram back to the parks.
Clue 7: Spot Mickey on a pole.
2 points

*
Make your way back to Downtown Disney, then walk over to **Disney's Grand Californian Hotel & Spa**.

Disney's Grand Californian Hotel & Spa
(79 points)

*
Look around outside the main entrance.

Clue 8: Search for Mickey's full face on a panel.
5 points

Clue 9: In this same area, find classic Mickeys on four different panels.
5 points for four or more

*
Now enter the lobby.
Clue 10: Search low for a Hidden Mickey on a rug. (This rug disappears at times to be cleaned.)
3 points

Clue 11: Study the front of the main registration counters for a "conductor Mickey."
5 points

Clue 12: Now search the front of these registration counters nearby for a classic Mickey.
4 points

Clue 13: Finally, search the front of the registration counters one last time for a Hidden Tinker Bell.
5 points

Clue 14: Glance behind the main registration counters for a classic Mickey on a tree.
4 points

Clue 15: Look for two other classic Mickeys behind the main registration counters.
4 points for finding both

Clue 16: Search the other registration counter at the far left (as you face the main registration counter) for three Hidden Mickeys.
5 points for finding all three

Clue 17: Ask a Cast Member at one of the lobby counters to show you a "Disney's Grand Californian Hotel & Spa" writing pen. Study it for a Hidden Mickey!
5 points

Clue 18: This Hidden Mickey knows what time it is!
5 points

Clue 19: Spot a Mickey image on a desk.
3 points

Clue 20: Find Mickey on a map.
3 points

Clue 21: Look for Mickey on a wall in the hallway with the restrooms not far from the registration counters.
3 points

Clue 22: Search for Mickey near the fireplace.
3 points

Clue 23: Just outside the exit doors near and to the rear of the fireplace is a Hidden Mickey similar to the one ab
ove.
3 points

*
  Enter the *Hearthstone Lounge*.

Clue 24: Check around for a Hidden Mickey.
2 points
If you're hungry, snack inside Hearthstone Lounge or try to get seated for lunch at Storytellers Cafe.

*
  Stroll through the exit doors that lead to *Downtown Disney*.

Clue 25: Look up and to your right for a Hidden Mickey.
3 points

* Return to the main lobby and take the exit that leads to *Disney California Adventure Park*.

Clue 26: After a few steps, look up for Mickey.
3 points

Clue 27: Now locate Mickey close to the walkway.
2 points

* Head back to the Grand Californian lobby once more and stroll out the front entrance to Disneyland Drive (which will take you over to *Disney's Pixar Place Hotel* if you are up for more Mickey hunting now).

Clue 28: Find Mickey on a sign.
2 points

Clue 29: Search for Mickey bike racks.
2 points

* When you are ready to continue your Mickey sleuthing, stroll over to **Disney's Pixar Place Hotel**.

Disney's Pixar Place Hotel
(3 points)

* Search outside the front of the hotel.
Clue 30: <u>Discover a Hidden Mickey in the bushes!</u>
3 points

* Gaze south from an upper floor.

Clue 31: If you can access an upper floor to look south along Disneyland Drive, you might be able to make out two sidewalks that outline a classic Mickey. (Or, zoom into the image on Google Earth).
5 bonus points

*
Your final stop: the ***Disneyland Hotel***.

Disneyland Hotel
(59 points)

*
Check out the area outside the front entrance.

Clue 32: Spot Hidden Mickeys in the nearby parking lot.
1 point

Clue 33: While you're at the hotel entrance, don't miss Mickey on the luggage carts.
1 point

*
Step into the lobby.
Clue 34: Search for tiny Hidden Mickeys in the registration lobby.
3 points

Clue 35: Find Mickey facing the main lobby elevators.
3 points

Clue 36: Study the mirrored glass walls inside the elevators for Mickey.
3 points

*
Return to the main lobby.

Clue 37: Study nearby telephones for Hidden Mickeys.
2 points

*
Now look around the hotel complex to find more Hidden Mickeys.

Clue 38: Spot a Hidden Mickey in the ***Convention Center*** area.
2 points

129

Clue 39: Search the ceiling near **Goofy's Kitchen** for Hidden Mickeys.
5 points for five Hidden Mickeys

Clue 40: Don't overlook Mickey on the stair handrail!
1 point

Clue 41: Look up for two Mickey images above the top of a staircase.
4 points for both

Clue 42: Up the escalator from *Goofy's Kitchen*, find a painting of Toontown on the wall and study it to spot two Hidden Mickeys.
4 points for finding both

Clue 43: In a painting nearby of a *Splash Mountain* scene, look for three Hidden Mickeys.
5 points for spotting all three

Clue 44: Locate a painting of *Space Mountain*. It has a Hidden Mickey, too!
3 points

Clue 45: Stroll the hotel hallways near the Sleeping Beauty Pavilion for Hidden Mickeys at your feet.
2 points for one or more

Clue 46: Near the Sleeping Beauty Pavilion, scrutinize a painting of a jungle temple for a Hidden Mickey.
5 points

*Walk into the **Frontier Tower** lobby.
Clue 47: Find furniture in a Mickey shape.
2 points

Clue 48: In the lobby, search for a tiny classic Mickey in a display.
5 points

Clue 49: Near the *Frontier Tower* lobby, locate classic Mickeys on a dress.
4 points

Clue 50: Also near the lobby, look for a painting with two Mickey hats.
4 points for both

Time now to see how you did.

Total Points for Downtown Disney and the Resort Hotels =

How'd You Do?

Up to 63 points - Bronze
64 to 126 points - Silver
127 points and over - Gold
158 points - Perfect Score

You may have done even better if you earned bonus points with the sidewalk Hidden Mickey on Disneyland Drive.

If you need help, the Hints are here for you!

Downtown Disney District

(Note: Disney may close one or more of the Downtown Disney stores mentioned below to make way for new experiences).

- *Splitsville Luxury Lanes*

Hint 1: Inside *Splitsville Luxury Lanes*, look around the lower level for a classic Hidden Mickey on the wall. It's formed of holes in a large orange in a mural – entitled "Welcome to Golden Lanes" – painted on the wall on the right of the bowling lanes.

133

Hint 2: Another classic Hidden Mickey is at the lower left of an upper level mural – entitled "Greetings from Splitsville @ Downtown Disney District" – and is made by finger holes in a brown bowling ball.

- Marceline's Confectionery

Hint 3: On the sign in front of the store, swirls in the letters "M" and "C" combine to form a classic Mickey.

- Kiosks near the entrance plaza

Hint 4: The eaves of several kiosks sport classic Mickey-shaped supports.

Mickey & Friends Parking Structure
- Walkway near the tram stop

Hint 5: On the walkway near the tram stop, a classic Mickey sits atop the sign that points the way to *Mickey & Friends Parking Structure* and the other parking areas. (You can find these classic Mickeys atop other signposts around Disneyland Resort property).

- Inside the parking structure

Hint 6: Inside the parking garage next to the security checkpoint area, classic Mickeys adorn the light fixtures hanging from the ceiling.

- Tram to the parks

Hint 7: Classic Mickeys top the light poles that line the tram path from the *Mickey & Friends Parking Structure* to the parks. (You can spot these light pole Mickeys in other areas around the Disneyland Resort property, such as in some of the parking lots.)

Disney's Grand Californian Hotel & Spa

- *Outside the main entrance*

Hint 8: A pillar just outside the main entrance is covered with colorful panels. On the rear panel, a three-quarter image of Mickey's face looks out from between the outer branches of a tree. He's about three quarters of the way up the left side of the tree.

Hint 9: On this same rear panel, a classic Mickey is at the middle bottom of the tree, just above the trunk. A second classic Mickey is in another tree at the upper right of the panel. In fact, you can spot small classic Mickeys in some of the trees on all four panels around this pillar!

- *Lobby area and nearby hallways*

Hint 10: As you enter the *Grand Californian* lobby, look for a rug with the hotel's tree logo to spot the small classic Mickey above the tree's trunk. This rug disappears at times to be cleaned. (Wherever you come across the *Grand Californian Hotel* logo, you're likely to spot a classic Mickey in the lower middle of the tree branches.)

Hint 11: A small side view of Mickey Mouse is sculpted in tile on the front desk. Toward the middle of the long counter, look for dancing bears on a panel in a depression in the desk. Mickey Mouse is conducting with a wand to the right of the white bear.

Hint 12: To the right of "conductor Mickey" is a raised, brown and green classic Mickey on the lower middle part of a tree.

Hint 13: To the left of "conductor Mickey" is a figure of Tinker Bell near (and to the immediate left of) a flat, dark writing surface.

Hint 14: On a fabric mural on the far left side of the rear wall behind the main registration counters, a dark classic Mickey hides just above the trunk in the branches of the leftmost tree.

Hint 15: You can spot two classic Mickeys on the left side of a fabric mural that hangs on the far right side of the rear wall behind the main registration counters. One is below the second maroon line from the top and the other is above the fifth maroon line from the top.

Hint 16: On the registration counter to the far left (as you face the main registration counters), look for ceramic green trees on each side of the front of the counter. Classic Mickeys are in their lower branches. A third classic Mickey sits in the lower middle branches of a tiny light-yellow tree to the upper left of the green tree on the right side of the counter.

Hint 17: Disneyland Resort's smallest Hidden Mickey is on a writing pen labeled with "Disney's Grand Californian Hotel & Spa." The tiny classic Mickey is on the tree logo for the hotel, at the bottom middle of the tree limbs.

Hint 18: A classic Mickey depression is on the face of the grandfather clock in the main lobby.

Hint 19: A classic Mickey hole is in the middle front of a desk, high up under the projecting lip of the desktop. The desk is often in the lobby - rear left.

Hint 20: On a map of the *Grand Californian* on a wall along a walkway at the left (as you enter) of the main lobby, the Children's Pool area is shaped like a classic Mickey.

Hint 21: In the nearby hallway to the left of the main entrance (as you face in from the entrance), classic Mickeys are in the corners of the frame of a painting that hangs on the wall near the restrooms. The painting shows a rocky and mountainous coastline.

Hint 22: A classic Mickey made of round stones and tilted to the right is in the lower front part of the rock wall on the left side of the lobby fireplace.

Hint 23: Another classic Mickey made of round rocks is in the wall to your right as you walk out the exit doors near and to the rear of the fireplace. A crack crosses Mickey's "head," which is in the second row from the top of the rock pile and four rocks back from the far edge of the wall. The classic Mickey is tilted to the right, almost sideways.

- Hearthstone Lounge

Hint 24: Classic Mickey holes repeat near the outer rim of some of the large light fixtures on the walls and hanging from the ceiling in the *Hearthstone Lounge*.

- Walkway to Downtown Disney

Hint 25: As you start along the walkway to Downtown Disney District, turn to your right and look up to spot a classic Mickey on the *Grand Californian* logo tree in an upper-story window.

- *Walkway to Disney California Adventure*

Hint 26: The side panels of the lamps along the walkway to the Disney California Adventure Park entrance are embellished with tree designs. The tallest tree on each panel has a classic Mickey at the bottom center of the tree limbs.

Hint 27: Classic Mickeys adorn each of the *Grand Californian* tree logos that are embossed on the planters lining the walkway.

- *Disneyland Drive*

Hint 28: The large *Grand Californian* entrance signs facing Disneyland Drive include the hotel's tree logo with its classic Mickey.

Hint 29: As you face the *Grand Californian Hotel* from Disneyland Drive, look for a Cast Member entrance driveway to the right of the main entrance to the hotel. Bicycle racks shaped as classic Mickeys are along the left side of this driveway.

Disney's Pixar Place Hotel

- *Outside the hotel*

Hint 30: A classic Mickey is on top of a green pole in front of the hotel, by the check-in parking spaces. This pole (with electrical sockets) is hidden in bushes.

- *Inside the hotel from Upper Floors*

Hint 31: This classic Mickey takes its shape from two sidewalks on either side of Disneyland Drive approaching Katella Avenue. The sidewalks themselves provide the outline, and you can really only see it from above. Trees planted near the sidewalks may obscure the image from overhead. You might be able to spot the image from upper floors in *Pixar Place Hotel*. Otherwise, you can admire it from the air or on Google Earth.

Disneyland Hotel

- *Lobby and entrance areas*

Hint 32: Classic Mickeys top the light poles in the main entrance parking lot.

Hint 33: Classic Mickeys are hiding in the middle of the side railings of the luggage carts.

Hint 34: In the lobby, several blue rectangular panels decorate the front of the long registration counter. These panels contain many tiny bubbles of different sizes that form classic Mickeys at intervals.

Hint 35: A wall covered with photographs faces the main lobby elevators. Above right of the large photo of Walt Disney with a map of Disneyland is a photo of Walt leaning out of a train; he's holding a large Mickey doll.

Hint 36: On the mirrored glass on the left side wall of the elevators (as you face the doors from inside), a small white classic Mickey hides in the stars near the elevator doors.

Hint 37: Back upstairs, the telephones in the hallways near the central lobby sport classic Mickeys above one of the touchtone buttons at the bottom of the phones.

- Around the hotel complex

Hint 38: Inside the hotel, in the *Convention Center* area to the right, you can usually find classic Hidden Mickeys in the carpet.

Hint 39: To the right of *Goofy's Kitchen* and *Steakhouse 55,* umbrellas hanging from the ceiling sport classic Hidden Mickeys.

Hint 40: Gold classic Mickeys are atop the ends of the middle handrail on the stairs near *Goofy's Kitchen.*

Hint 41: On the ceiling at the top of a staircase near *Goofy's Kitchen*, a large classic Mickey on a blue background is secured by small classic Mickey bolts.

Hint 42: Find the woman wearing a red dress in the right lower section of a stylized painting of Toontown. The two children with her are wearing Mickey ears.

Hint 43: Look at the lower right section of the painting of a scene in front of *Splash Mountain*. From left to right, you can spot three classic Mickeys: a red Mickey balloon, a small white and black Mickey balloon, and, at the far right of the painting, a child with Mickey ears.

Hint 44: Glance around for a painting of *Space Mountain*. In the sky at the upper left is a fireworks classic Mickey tilted to the left.

- Near Sleeping Beauty Pavilion

Hint 45: Classic Mickeys are in the carpet in the hallways near the Sleeping Beauty Pavilion and the Magic Kingdom Ballroom.

Hint 46: Across from the Sleeping Beauty Pavilion, a classic Mickey hides in a painting of a jungle temple. It's on the top front of the hood of a jeep at the lower middle of the painting.

- Frontier Tower Lobby

Hint 47: In the *Frontier Tower* Lobby, ottomans are often arranged in a classic Mickey formation. You'll sometimes find the same arrangement in the *Fantasy and Adventure Towers*.

Hint 48: In the lobby is a miniature concept model of the *Big Thunder Mountain Railroad* attraction in Disneyland. Along the rear side of the display, you can spot the three-gear classic Mickey by the track, representing the real classic Mickey gears on the park ride. The gear Hidden Mickey sits on the ground near a wooden tower.

Hint 49: In a hallway to the left of the lobby, check out the right wall next to the stairwell for a painting of a steamboat landing. In its foreground, a woman walks with two children. Her dress has a classic Mickey pattern.

Hint 50: In the stairwell itself (leading down from the hallway to the left of the Frontier Tower lobby), look for a painting with the word "Frontierland." A child in a train car in the middle of the painting is wearing Mickey ears, as is a man in the stagecoach at the top of the painting.

Chapter 5

Other Mickey Appearances

These Hidden Mickeys won't earn you any points, but you're bound to enjoy them if you're in the right place at the right time to see them.

Look for holiday Hidden Mickeys if you're at Disneyland during the Christmas season, or for that matter, any major holiday.

Other "Hidden" Mickeys - decor and deliberate - appear with some regularity throughout the Disneyland Resort. Notice the Mickster on Disneyland brochures, maps and flags, Cast Member name tags, Cast Member uniforms, guest room keys, telephones and phone books, and restaurant and store receipts. The restaurants sometimes offer classic Mickey butter and margarine pats, pancakes and waffles, and pizzas and pasta, as well as Mickey napkins. They also arrange dishes and condiments to form classic Mickeys. Some condiment containers are even shaped like Mickey. You might notice classic Mickey holes in the backs of some high chairs. Road signs on Disneyland property may sport Mickey ears, and Disneyland vehicles and monorails may display Mickey Mouse insignia.

Cleaning personnel will often spray the ground, windows, furniture, and other items with three circles of cleaning solution (a classic Mickey) before the final cleansing. Or they may leave three wet Mickey Mouse circles or other Disney character images on the pavement after mopping! Mickey even decorates manhole covers, survey markers, and utility covers in the ground, as you've probably already discovered for yourself.

Enjoy all these Mickeys as you experience Disneyland. And if you want to take some home with you, rest assured that you can usually find "Hidden" Mickeys on souvenir mugs, merchandise bags and boxes, T-shirts, and Christmas tree ornaments sold in the Disneyland shops. So even when you're far away from Disneyland, you can continue to enjoy Hidden Mickeys.

To marvel at a Hidden Mickey from above, check out Google Earth and find the classic Mickey created by two sidewalks on either side of Disneyland Drive approaching Katella Avenue— below and just to the right of Disney's Pixar Place Hotel in the Google Earth image. The sidewalks form a distorted Mickey image, but the voters on my website liked it as a Hidden Mickey. I hope you will, too.

To access the image, go to Google Earth (you can download the free Google Earth program), type in "Disneyland, California," and click on the "Search" button next to the destination. Then scroll with your mouse to the left and down until you're just below the Pixar Place hotel, and you'll see the palm-outlined Hidden Mickey. (The palm-lined sidewalks form the head and ears). You may have to play around with the dials on your screen to get a good view. (Note: The trees are covering up the image more and more in recent years.)

Chapter 6

My Favorite Hidden Mickeys

In this field guide, I've described more than 415 Hidden Mickeys at the Disneyland Resort. I enjoy every one of them, but the following are extra special to me. They're special because of their uniqueness, their deep camouflage (which makes them especially hard to find), or the "Eureka!" response they elicit when I spot them—or any combination of the above. Here then are my Favorite Hidden Mickeys at Disneyland. I apologize to you if your favorite Hidden Mickey is not (yet) on the list below.

My Top Ten

1. Conductor Mickey. Check the registration counter at Disney's Grand Californian Hotel & Spa and marvel at this magnificent (but tiny) rendition of Mickey conducting an imagined musical symphony for the dancing bears nearby. You'll feel like singing along! (Clue 11, Chap. 4)

2. Randall's Mickey. In the *Monster's Inc.* ride, Hollywood Land, Disney California Adventure Park, the little girl Boo pounds monster Randall with a bat. As Randall (who looks like a lizard and changes color like a chameleon) changes colors, a classic Mickey sometimes appears on his belly. This great Mickey image is intermittent, so stare long and

hard at poor Randall, and don't wince!
(Clue 58, Chap. 3)

3. Mountain Snow Mickey, Disneyland
Park. There's more than snow on the
Disneyland Matterhorn! Admire the ma-
jestic mountain from near "it's a small
world" for a Mickey clearing in the snow.
(Clue 8, Chap. 2)

4. Mr. Toad's Door Mickey, Fantasyland, Disneyland Park. You mustn't
miss this marvelous Mickey image on
the right door (lower left corner) of the
third set of doors you crash through at
the beginning of *Mr. Toad's Wild Ride*.
Try not to wreck your car looking for it!
(Clue 98, Chap. 2)

5. 1901 Lounge Doorman Mickey, Buena
Vista Street, Disney California Adventure. A tiny Mickey below your feet
greets you at the door, wishing you swell
times ahead! (Clue 107, Chap. 3)

6. Pirate-Armor Mickey, New Orleans
Square, Disneyland. It must've been
one proud pirate who wore this Mickey
armor breastplate which you'll find on
Pirates of the Caribbean. I feel a song
coming on: "Yo, ho, yo, ho, a pirate's life
for me." (Clue 37, Chap. 2)

7. Purple Car-Hood Mickey. This faint
white classic Mickey on a car hood
inside Ramone's House of Body Art in
Cars Land, Disney California Adventure,
is a clever touch by the artist. You may
need help from a Cast Member to find it!
(Clue 99, Chap. 3)

8. Winnie the Pooh's Tree Mickey.
As you take off in your beehive in *The
Many Adventures of Winnie the Pooh*,
Critter Country, Disneyland Park, squint
to your right to admire this subtle classic

Mickey in the bark of a tree. When you see it, you'll want to bounce like Tigger! (Clue 148, Chap. 2)

9. Big Ben Mickey. A side view of Mickey's face is below you in a window of Big Ben during *Peter Pan's Flight* in Disneyland's Fantasyland. Look back to spot Mickey in London! (Clue 5, Chap. 2)

10. Mark Twain Mickey. Make a special trip to Frontierland, Disneyland Park, to find a painting of Mickey on a steamboat. He's standing by two well-dressed women on the lower deck of the *Mark Twain Riverboat*. Mickey in a tux! (Clue 118, Chap. 2)

Ten Honorable Mentions

11. Nemo Rock Mickey. Make a special effort to chase down this classic Mickey in a rock wall in Tomorrowland, Disneyland Park, near both the elevator for the *Disneyland Monorail* and *Finding Nemo Submarine Voyage*. You won't regret it! (Clue 142, Chap. 2)

12. Pinocchio Ship Mickey. Pinocchio is a classic, and so is this hard-to-spot, elegant classic Mickey on a model ship's case in *Pinocchio's Daring Journey*, Fantasyland, Disneyland. Ahoy, Mickey! (Clue 109, Chap. 2)

13. *Mickey & Minnie's Runaway Railway* clam Mickey. This attraction in Mickey's Toontown, Disneyland, is filled to the brim with Hidden Mickeys! One of the best is the clam pearl classic Mickey at the bottom of the waterfall. It appears for only a split second! (Clue 60, Chap. 2)

14. Still-life Painting Mickey, Emporium store, Disneyland Park. You may need to step up close to the painting, as this Sorcerer Mickey almost escapes detection! (Clue 178, Chap. 2)

15. Jungle Painting Mickey, Disneyland Hotel. Search this painting on a wall across from the Sleeping Beauty Pavilion for a Hidden Mickey you might encounter while on a wild expedition. (Clue 46, Chap. 4)

16. Lava Mickey. Along the *Toy Story Midway Mania* ride, Pixar Pier, Disney California Adventure, don't overlook Mickey in the lava behind a middle-level balloon. You have to pop the balloon to see Mickey. (Clue 16, Chap. 3)

17. *Guardians of the Galaxy: Mission: BREAKOUT!* Avengers Campus, Disney California Adventure. Wow! A tiny classic Mickey greets you on the left side of the screen showing the generator control room. Squint hard for this one! (Clue 10, Chap. 3)

18. *Radiator Springs Racers'* Electrical Mickey, Cars Land, Disney California Adventure. As you motor along, be quick for this Hidden Mickey on an electrical box in Ramone's Body Art shop. Don't worry, if you meet Luigi instead, you can admire Hidden Mickeys behind Luigi and on a red toolbox to your right. (Clues 3, 4, and 5, Chap. 3)

19. Schmoozies Minnie. We can't forget Minnie Mouse! At Schmoozies in Disney California Adventure's Hollywood Land, Minnie looks positively regal as the Statue of Liberty. (Clue 82, Chap. 3)

20. *Alice in Wonderland*, Fantasyland, Disneyland. Dive down the rabbit hole, but keep your eyes open for a tiny classic Mickey inside a window of the White Rabbit's house! (Clue 94, Chap. 2)

Don't Stop Now! ......

Hidden Mickey mania is contagious. The benign pastime of searching out Hidden Mickeys has escalated into a bona fide vacation mission for many Disneyland fans. I'm happy to add my name to the list of hunters. Searching for images of the Main Mouse can enhance a solo trip to the parks or a vacation for the entire family. Little ones delight in spotting and greeting Mickey Mouse characters in the parks and restaurants. As children grow, the Hidden Mickey game is a natural evolution of their fondness for the Mouse.

Join the search! With alert eyes and mind, you can spot Hidden Mickey classics and new ones waiting to be found. Even beginners can happen upon a new, unreported Hidden Mickey or two. As new attractions open and older ones get refurbished, new Hidden Mickeys await discovery.

The Disney entertainment phenomenon is unique in many ways, and Hidden Mickey mania is one manifestation of Disney's universal appeal. Join in the fun! Maybe I'll see you at Disneyland, marveling (like me) at the Hidden Gems. They're waiting patiently for you to discover them.

Acknowledgements .....

No Hidden Mickey hunter works alone. While I've spotted most of the Hidden Mickeys in this book on my own—and personally verified every single one of them—finding Hidden Mickeys is an ongoing group effort. I am indebted to the following dedicated Hidden Mickey explorers for alerting me to a number of Hidden Mickeys I might otherwise have missed. Thanks to each and every one of you for putting me on the track of one or more of these Disneyland treasures and, in some cases, also helping me verify them.

Those named in bold letters have spotted 10 or more, which includes current as well as lost Hidden Mickeys.

Extra special thanks to Rosemary and Neil (FindingMickey.com) for spotting and helping me verify over 200 Hidden Mickeys at Disneyland **and to Sharon Dale and Sharon Gee** for finding over 50.

Karlos Aguilera, Jonathan Agurcia, Kala'i Ahlo-Souza, The Alberti's, David Almanza, Kirsty Alsop, Antonio Altamirano, James Amato, Bob Anderson, Katrina Andrews, A.J. Apellido, Issac Aragon, Vahe Arevshatian, Cheryl Armstrong, John Axtell, Kristi B., Ori B., **Brian Babcock, Kim Bacon and Family,** Duane Baker, Jennifer Baker, Ruby Beatrice Baker, Hans Balders, Matt and Shelly and Keira Barbieri, Andrew Bardsley, Katharine & Ammon Barney, Daniel Barrach, Melissa Barrett, Melisa Beardslee, Bradly Behmer, **April Beisser,** Richard Beltran, John Benavidez II, Daniel and Elise Berdin,

Brian Bergstrom, Dessa Bernabe, Jenny Bigpond, **Murray Bishop,** Tina Blaylock, Tyler and Brandie Bolton, Tim Bonanno, Cam Bondoc, Jacob Steven Bonillas, Corey Borgen, Lynn Boyd, Lori Brackett, Chad Bradbury, Erik Bratlien, Vicky Braun, David Breede, Rod Brouhard, Carol Brown, Kaden Brown, Keller Brown, Nicolas Brown, Peter Brown, Thierry and Gabriella and Matthieu Bruxelle, Colin Buchanan, Michael Buell, Fernando Bueno, Josh Burch, Marjorie Burns, Felix Bustos, Nate Buteyn, Amy C., Peter C., Ashley Cabrera, Chris Caflisch, Bev Cain, Stacy Campbell, Craig Canady, Marisa Cardenas, Nicholas Noah Carreno, Peter Cefalu, Gail Chambers, Leonard Chan, Austin Chanu, Danielle Chard, Chelsi Chipps, Emmy Christopherson, Diana Cimadamore, John Clover, Alan Coffman, Mary Jo Collins, Jeffrey Colwell, Catherine Conroy, Emily Cook and brother, Megan Cook, Dee Cook-Whitlatch, Michelle Cornelius, **Sherrie Cotton,** Marissa Covarrubias, **Josh and Cassi Cox,** The Coylar Family, Michael Cross, **Sharon Dale,** Erika Davila, Carlos A. de Alba, Jessica de la Vara, Jess Delgado, Justin DeMartini, Mike Demopoulos, Jeremiah Dempsey, Jacob DePriest, Tim Devine, Matt Dickerson, Casey Dietz, Thea Dodge, Phillip Donnelly, Tom Donnelly, Jaime Doyle, Maria Dufault, Madison Dunn, Lindsey E., Michael Early, Kyle Edison, Chad Elliot, John Emmert, Scott Evans, Victor Evora, Miranda Michelle Felice, Joel Feria, Jennifer Fernandez, Troy and Cheyanne Field, Rob Fitzpatrick, Nicholas Fleming, Joe Flowers, Melissa Forte, Keitaro Francisco, Matthew Furstenfeld, Ben G., Robert Gainor, Curt Gale, **Jason Gall,** Ryan Gall, Michele Galvez, Jon Gambill, Joshua Garces, Valerie Garren, **Sharon Gee,** Sam Gennawey, Amy Gervais,

Staci Gleed, Tyler Glynn, Alec Goldberg, Jimmy Golden, Micheline Golden, Reyna Gonzalez, Jeremiah Good, Jordan Goodman, Alex Goslar, Tim Grassey, Michael Greening, Christine Griffith, Josh Grothem, Werner Grundlingh, Kimberly Gryte, Carl H., Dave H., Elaine H., Josh and Alyssa and Melody Hadeen, Michael Hadlock, Holly Haider, John Hall, Sarah Hall, The Hallak Family, Rachel Hammond, Brian Hancock, Jon Handler, Chris Hansen, Cynthia Hess, Kate Heylman, Alec Hickman, **Mari Highleyman,** Carl Hoffman, Paul Hoffman, **Milton Holecek,** Michael Hollingsworth, **Ethan Holmes**, Chas Howell, Cory Hughes, Robert Huntington, Bill Iadonisi, Malaine Ivy-Decker, Tara Jacob, Molly Jane, Sharise Jaso, Loren Javier, **Mike Johansen,** James Johnson, Amy Jones, Michelle June, Gordon K., Matt K., Tom K., Summer Kane, Jennifer Kanihan, Andranik Karapetian, **Mehlanie Kayra,** Ryan Kehoe, Della Kingsland, Xela Knarf,   Andrew Knight, Matthew and Missy Knoll, Keri Kruger, Dalia Kuarez, Meghan Kueny-Thornburg, Jackie Kushnier, Chase L., Christine Lamar, Kimberly Lamb, Rhonda Lampitt, Ledawn Larsen, Cortney Laurence, Martin Lee, Phillip Lemon, Andrew Lepire, Tony Lepore, Annie Lin, Ronald Lindberg, Alysia Lippetti, Myrna Litt, Ryan Lizama, Lourdes Llanes, Allison Lloyd, Joe Loecsey, Amber Lopez, Brian Z. Lucas, Katherine Lugo, Sal Lugo, Thao Luong, Austin M., Christina M., Henry Macall, Heather Mackey, Hank Mahler, Maria Maki, C. Mallonee, Cori Mallonee, Dawn Maple, Jorge Mario, Jasmine Martinez, John Martinez, Juan M. Martinez Ill, Paul Martinez, Dave Marx, **Michael Mason,** Kim McClaughry, Krystle McClung, Ciara McGovern, James Mcguine, Cindy McKeown, Connor McKeown,

Sylvia McNeil, Oscar Mejorado, Bill and Kari Middeke, Anthony Miele, Phoebe Mikalonis, Justine Mikhail, The Miles Family, Dallas Millam, Randi Miller, Robert Miller, Amanda Mitton, Kotomi Miyajima, Sandy Montelongo, Robert Montiel, Christopher Morales, Jose Moran, Carlos Moreno, Rebecca Mortin, Danny Mui, The Muklewicz Family, Tom Nadzieja, Lindsey Naizer, **Bobby Naus,** Kristen Naus, Andy Neitzert, A. Nelson, Aly Nelson, Aryn Nelson, J. Nelson, Marina Nelson, Dave and Kim Ness, Jay Nicholson, Ty Nielson, Daniel Nieto, Joseph Nolan, Jen O'Bryan, Elaine Oje-da, Michael and Wendy Olayvar, Jennifer Oliphant, Gillian O'Neal, Ryan Ong, Orlando Attractions magazine, **Steve Orme,** Greg Ostravich, Jessica Out-het, Andrew P., Joey P., Monica Garcia Montero P., Sam P., Priscilla Padilla, Shawna Park, Steve Parmley, Justin Parnell, Anika Patel, Cherna Patterson, Winston Peacock, Mark Pellegrini, Brian A. Pellowski, Cheyenne Pemberton, Rob and Buffy and Anna and Julia Penttila, Jennifer Peterson, Christopher Phelan, Leslie Phillips, Eric Polk, Roger Pollard, Diana Poncini, Heather Pone, Robert Powers, Kaitlyn Pratt, Melanie Price, Alyssa Proudfoot, Carlos Quintanilla, Marv R., Louise Rafferty, BJ Ralphs, Angel Ramirez, Sal Ramirez, Brendan Ratner, Sara Reid, Caleb Richards, Leslie Richards, Linda Richards, Marv Richards, Alex Roake, Jacob Robbins, Max Roberts, Joy E. Robertson-Fin-ley, Jeff Robinson, Jose Rodriguez, Katie Rogers, Geoff Rogos, George Rojas, Shaun Rosen, Lucas Ross, Todd Rosspencer, Jean Rowley, Angie Royce, Julian Rucki, Jessica Ruggles, Caleb Ruiz, Richard Ruiz, **Russ Rylee,** John Salinas, Ron Salinas, Jennifer Sal-vatierra, Dominic Sanna, Bianca and Nathan and Isaac Santoro, Brandie

Sargent, Candace and Emily and Ethan Sauter, Andy Schelb, Kaleigh Schiro, **Zod Schultz**, P. Schwarz, Tony "Bonz" Sciortino, Chris Scott, Kira Scott, Tim Scott, Lauren Seibert, Lisa Sentif, Khrys Sganga, The Shank Family, Nate Sharp, Michael Shearin, Mark Sheppard, The Sherrick Family, Derek Shimozaki, Ryan Shimozaki, Heather Sievers, Zach Simes, Amy Simpson, Shannan Sinclair, Nick Skiles, Breana Nicole Smith, Rebecca Smith, Jose Solano, Christopher Solesbee, Braden Stanley, Brad Steinbrenner, Lloyd Stevens, Anastasia Stewart, Darrell St. Pierre, Taylor Stratton, Chris Strodder (author of "The Disneyland Book of Lists"), Jessica Strom, Tyler Struck, Rich Sylvester, Erin T., Mitch T., Stacy T., Donna Taing, Mark Talle, Stacy Tanaka, Pat Tee, Nikolas Tejeda, Mark Temte, Nancy Terrazas, Craig R. Thompson, Darin Thompson, Sheryl Thompson, Joseph Thorne, Sandy Thornton, Andrew Thorp, The Tierney Family, Tim Titus, Micaela Tracy, Mark Treiger, Amy and Donnie Triphan, The Trujillo Family, Shantelle Ullery (Instagram @disneylandtourguide), Karen Ullman (and her Storybook Land Guide), Eric Upah, Christian Urcia, **Luis Valdez,** Ryan Valle, Kim Vander Dussen, Sam Vanderspek, Jessica Van Linge, Jeff Van Ry, Aldo Velez, Evelyn Vides, Juliet Violette, Fred Vosecky, Heather W., Ron W., Brock Waidmann, Mel Waidmann III, Melvin Waidmann II, Rhonda Waidmann, William Waidmann, Barrie & Jack Waldman-Marker, Chris Walhof, Scott and Kate Walker, Matt Walsh, Yvonne Washburn, Bud Webb, Sharla Webb, Austin Weber, Angela Welliver, Carolyn Whiteford, Christopher Williams, Deb Wills, Ken Wilson, Emily Woods, Gracie Wright, Jack Wright, Laura Wright, Jeanine Yamanaka, Lynn Yaw, Justin Yert,

Tammy York, Ava Z., and Monique Zimmer.

AND

AJ, Alan, Alex, Alexa, Alexz, Amanda, Amber, Amy, Angel, Ari, Audrey, Austin, BP, Brittany, Burley, Cathy, Celandra, Cherna, Chris, Christopher, C.J., C.K., Claire, Cole, Cori, Daniel, Danny, Dee, Derrick, Destiny, Dianna, disneyland21, DVC Cast Member, Elizabeth, Emily, Emmett, Eric, **Eric and Colleen and Julie,** ES, Evan, Hans, Hayden, Hayley, Heather, **Helen and Danny,** Imp, Informer, JC, Jen, Jessica, Jonathan, Josh, Julie, Justin, Kayleigh, Kelsey, Kendra, Kevin, Kim, Krister, Kristen and family, KS and CK, Laura, Laura and Lily, Laura and Memoree, Lea Ann, Lloyd, LMD Hidden Mickey Finders, Lori, Luke, Mari, Mark, Matt, Matt@OrlandoAttractionsMagazine, Matthew, Meg, Megan, Melissa, Michaela, Mike, M. L., Morgan, Nathan, Nicky, Nitza, Nix, Nolan, Nusy, Olivia, Peter, Pinky, Queenkoalaandme, Rachel, RaeLynn, Rhonda, **Rosemary and Neil (FindingMickey.com),** Ryan, Sam, Sandy, Sara, Sarah, Sawyer, Scott, Seeing, Serena, Shannon, Shaun, Shirlyn, Stephanie, Sylvia, **Tamera,** Taylor, Teressa, Tia, Toneto and Laura and Steph, Tracy, Ty, Wayne, **Where's Mickey (myspace.com/wheresmickey),** Xander, Ylimegirl, Zod, and Zoe.

------- Index -------

Index to Mickey's Hiding Places

Note: This Index includes only those rides, restaurants, shops, hotels and other places in the Disneyland Resort that harbor confirmed Hidden Mickeys. If the attraction you're looking for isn't included, Mickey isn't hiding there. Or if he is, I haven't spotted him yet.

- Steve Barrett

The following abbreviations appear in this Index:
DL - Disneyland Park
CA - Disney California Adventure Park
DD - Downtown Disney District
RH - Resort Hotel

Page numbers refer to the Clues.

J

K

L

M

T

W